Bird Homes
and Habitats

Bird Homes and Habitats

Bill Thompson III

HOUGHTON MIFFLIN HARCOURT
BOSTON   NEW YORK   2013

www.hmhbooks.com

Library of Congress Cataloging-in-Publication Data is available.
ISBN 978-0-618-90446-4

Book design by George Restrepo

Printed in China
SCP 10 9 8 7 6 5 4 3 2 1

The legacy of America's greatest naturalist and creator of the field guide series, Roger Tory Peterson, is kept alive through the dedicated work of the Roger Tory Peterson Institute of Natural History (RTPI). Established in 1985, RTPI is located in Peterson's hometown of Jamestown, New York, near the Chautauqua Institution in the southwestern part of the state.

Today RTPI is a national center for nature education that maintains, shares, and interprets Peterson's extraordinary archive of writings, art, and photography. The institute, housed in a landmark building by world-class architect Robert A. M. Stern, continues to transmit Peterson's zest for teaching about the natural world through leadership programs in teacher development as well as outstanding exhibits of contemporary nature art, natural history, and the Peterson Collection.

Your participation as a steward of the Peterson Collection and supporter of the Peterson legacy is needed. Please consider joining RTPI at an introductory rate of 50 percent of the regular membership fee for the first year. Simply call RTPI's membership department at 800-758-6841 ext. 226, or e-mail membership@rtpi.org to take advantage of this special membership offered to purchasers of this book. For more information, please visit the Peterson Institute in person or virtually at www.rtpi.org.

*For Julie Zickefoose, the most caring bird landlord
I know.*

*And for all those nest box trail operators and bird
gardeners across America: thank you for your time and
devotion to nesting birds.*

Contents

Acknowledgments

I HAVE BEEN PROVIDING nesting habitat and housing for birds for the past twenty-plus years, but there is always something more to know and new things to learn. So I don't consider myself an expert as much as a serious student of birds. My wife, Julie Zickefoose, *is* an expert on nesting birds and bird gardening, and I am indebted to her for all the years of sharing her knowledge with me. The thousands of birds that have hatched out of nest boxes or habitat on our farm are a testimony to Julie's passion and caring for the natural world.

My parents instilled a respect for nature in all of the Thompson kids, and they encouraged my interest in birds from the outset. My first memorable nesting-birds experience was watching the fledgling eastern screech-owls being fed outside my parents' bedroom window in Pella, Iowa. Mom and Dad knew that was really cool, and they let us stay up to watch the busy parents feed their owlets. Of course this was years before my folks started *Bird Watcher's Digest* in our living room. If you want to know about how *BWD* hatched, visit birdwatchersdigest.com and click on Our Story.

PURPLE CORNFLOWER *is a bird-friendly plant.*

Many longtime nest-box landlords and bird experts have shared their insight and information with me over the years. It's impossible to list them all here, but among the major influencers are: Lynn Barnhart, Dr. David Bird, Eirik A.T. Blom, Kevin Cook, Steve and Cheryl Eno, Steve Gilbertson, James R. Hill III, Alvaro Jaramillo, Doug Levasseur, Jim McCormac, Patricia Murphy, Bob Niebuhr, Bob Scott Placier, Darlene Sillick, Connie Toops, and Dick Tuttle.

I owe a bushel basket of thanks to the generous people who agreed to be profiled as Birdy Backyard All-Stars for this book. I pestered them all unmercifully. They are Dudley Edmondson, Steve and Cheryl Eno, Marci and Terry Fuller, Lynn Hassler, Alvaro Jaramillo, John and Durrae Johanek, Ed Kanze, Andy Kinsey, Alan Pulley, John Riutta, Clay and Pat Sutton, Connie and Pat Toops, Kathy Wiederholt, and Julie Zickefoose.

My wonderful colleagues at *Bird Watcher's Digest* make it possible for me to write books. And every now and then I catch someone here

NESTLING EASTERN bluebirds in a nest box made from PVC pipe.

at the *BWD* offices actually reading one of my books and this makes me really happy.

Any natural history book author dreams of being published by a company that really "gets" nature books. Time and again the talented people at Houghton Mifflin Harcourt make my writing into something that I can be proud of, truly. I feel lucky to be a Houghton author and to be edited by the amazing Lisa A. White. Among the many others at HMH to whom I owe a great deal are Beth Burleigh Fuller, Katrina Kruse, Taryn Roeder, and Brian Moore.

The peerless Elizabeth Pierson ran through the digital equivalent of many red pens in copyediting the three books in this series.

My agent, Russell Galen, is the oracle of the book business and I consider myself very fortunate to be one of his natural history clients.

Introduction

THE BOOK IN YOUR HANDS, *Bird Homes and Habitats*, is the third in a three-book series: Peterson Field Guide/*Bird Watcher's Digest* Backyard Bird Guides. This series is aimed at readers who hope to get more enjoyment out of watching birds and other wildlife in their backyards and gardens. I could try to encourage you to buy and read the first two books before diving into this one, but the truth is, the books work as well on their own as they do in a series. They are connected to—but not dependent on—one another. Having said that, I hope you will go buy the first two books! This book will be lonely without its two best friends. And the three books together look really wonderful on your bookshelf (or in your e-reader). Anyone noticing them will immediately recognize you as someone of impeccable taste, with a Zen-like hunger for greater backyard enlightenment. Trust me on this.

Everyone knows that if you want birds to come to your yard, you put out a bird feeder, or a birdhouse, and birds will show up. Simple, right? Well, yes and no. First of all, there are a zillion other things you can do to enhance the attractiveness of your landscape to birds and wildlife. Second, what if the birds you attract are not the ones you want? Anyone can put mixed seed in a tube feeder and get house sparrows and rock pigeons in droves. But these species are non-native and often drive more desirable, native birds away. What then?

That's why I'm here. As we journey together through the glittering prose that follows, we'll discover the solutions to the backyard mysteries of life. We'll look at nesting habitat for birds, at birdhouses, and at how to build, maintain, monitor, and enjoy them. We'll talk about the North American bird species that use nest boxes. And we'll learn how to deal with problems that arise in the backyard. We'll even meet some folks who are the creators of amazing backyard habitats for birds. Then you can steal all of their good ideas and apply them in your own backyard.

Are you ready? Great! Let's head out to the backyard and get going!
—BILL THOMPSON III

A HOUSE WREN pair courting and nest building in a wren house.

Bird Homes
and Habitats

HARSH WINTER weather makes the bird-feeding station extremely busy with visitors such as these American goldfinches.

Chapter 1: Bird-friendly Habitat

I'M SITTING HERE AT MY DESK, looking out the sliding glass door on the west side of our house. It's a cold, gray morning in early March—not the kind of day most of us would like to spend outdoors. Yet everywhere I look there are birds. Out under the Virginia pine cluster that I planted 15 years ago there are dark-eyed juncos, northern cardinals, mourning doves, blue jays, and a single male eastern towhee scratching through the pine needles and grass for some bits of mixed seed and cracked corn. Along the weedy edge of our old orchard, more juncos are foraging along with a song sparrow and several white-throated sparrows. Carolina chickadees and tufted titmice flit from the woods and hopscotch from the sumacs to the mulberry to the birch trees, and then to the bird feeders.

White-breasted nuthatches take one sunflower seed at a time over to the sycamore tree, where they wedge the seeds into a crack in a large branch and hammer them open. The peach tree we planted is just starting to show some swelling in the buds. It will be blooming just in time for the return of the ruby-throated hummingbirds in mid-April. American crows and a red-winged blackbird pick through the latest offerings on our compost pile. A pair of Carolina wrens is scold-singing at me as they bring billfulls of green moss to line their nest in the copper bucket above the front door. Red-bellied woodpeckers are hammering on both sides of the suet feeder—a male and a female and likely a mated pair. I watch as each flies off with a hunk of suet to cache for later consumption, perhaps near where they are excavating a nest hole for the coming breeding season.

THIS STAND of Virginia pines provides a sheltered place to feed the birds during a snowstorm.

All of these birds were here when we bought this old farm back in 1992, but they were nowhere near the house, which sits on a cleared ridgetop in the wooded hills of southeastern Ohio. At that time, the house had one or two shrubs near its foundation and acres of lawn in all directions. When we put up our first bird feeder, it sat unused

BRUSH PILES are easy to build and instantly make your yard more bird-friendly.

for weeks. When blustery weather came, the feeder swung back and forth in the wind until all of its seed was spilled out on the ground. Even then, no birds came to the feeder. I knew it was time to make some changes. The woodland birds may have noticed the feeder, but none of them was bold enough to cross 40 yards of open lawn to visit the feeder. Surely a Cooper's or sharp-shinned hawk would see them in the open and swoop down for the kill.

We started by moving the feeder farther from the house and closer to the woods. Halfway between the woodland edge and the feeder, I installed a large brush pile, which I created by dragging every dead branch I could find out from the woods. Hours later, the first Carolina chickadee perched on the tube feeder and removed a sunflower seed, taking it away hurriedly to the safety of the woods. In effect, the brush pile gave the songbirds a safe place to stop halfway to the feeders. They could perch there and scan for danger in all directions before proceeding to the feeder. We, and the birds, have never looked back. That one bit of habitat enhancement got us rolling. Now everything we do to the landscape outside our house is done to benefit the birds and enhance our ability to enjoy them.

Look outside at your backyard or garden. Is it offering the basic things that birds need? Not sure what those things are? It's fairly simple.

Four Things That All Birds Need

Birds require four elements in order to survive in any habitat: food, water, shelter, and a place to nest. They need food every day. Access to water is necessary on a regular basis, as is shelter, especially at night and during extreme weather. A place to nest is a breeding-season requirement, for without that birds cannot reproduce and keep their populations healthy and stable. Let's examine each of these elements in slightly greater detail.

FOOD

Birds require food on a daily basis in order to keep their "engine" running. A pygmy nuthatch or mountain chickadee may not survive a cold night if it can't eat enough to keep its metabolism operating, keeping it warm. A bird that cannot eat soon loses mobility, making it vulnerable to predators and weather extremes.

CEDAR WAXWINGS will flock to a fruit source such as this wild cherry tree.

We can provide food to our backyard birds in a variety of ways. The first and best way is naturally, by enhancing our landscape with plants that produce things that birds eat: seeds, fruits, plant matter, sap, and even the insects that come with a diverse habitat. Now, before you start worrying about having to become a master gardener, let me add that many bird-friendly plants are probably already part of your backyard landscape. When we moved to our farm in 1992, despite the fact that the previous owners kept everything mowed down below 2 inches in all directions, we still had lots of bird-friendly plants present along the woodland edge. Sassafras, sumac, wild grape, dogwoods, and other native trees were doing their part to feed the birds. What some might see as weeds—goldenrod, ironweed, milkweed, joe-pye weed, little bluestem, even crabgrass—we saw as natural bird feeders.

Take a visual seasonal inventory to see what grasses, flowers, shrubs, vines, and trees the birds seem to frequent. Even if you don't know the names of the plant species, you can tell which plants the birds use and allow more of them to grow. I did this on our farm when I dug up seedling Virginia pines along an old farm road that bisects our property and transplanted them on the edge of our yard. Those three trees are now 35 feet tall, and each fall and spring they are filled with migrant warblers. I know that many of our mourning doves roost in these pines.

A MOURNING dove on a platform feeder.

If you are still unsure about which plants are bird-friendly, get some professional help. In each of the first two books in this series, *Identifying and Feeding Birds* and *Hummingbirds and Butterflies* (which I coauthored with Connie Toops), there are lists of bird-friendly plants. Your state or provincial soil conservation service will have reference materials for your region. And there is a world of information available online. It helps in all plant searches to know which growing zone you are in so that you can select plants that will thrive in your regional average annual temperatures.

Plants and birds have developed a mutually beneficial relationship over the eons. Plants offer up their seeds to birds in the form of fruits, nuts, cones, and so forth. Birds find and consume these seeds. Once the seeds pass through the opposite end of the birds, they are ready to germinate, creating a new plant in a new location. Thus both birds and plants assist one another in their quest for survival. And this is why your local birds recognize your local plants as a source of food.

The second way we feed birds is by offering them food in feeders. Although this seems less natural than letting plants do all the work, if done properly, bird feeding can be equally symbiotic: birds get good, healthy food; we get the joy of seeing them at our feeders and the satisfaction of providing for them in some small way. The first book in this series, *Identifying and Feeding Birds,* offers up all you need to know about feeding birds, no matter where you live in North America. I won't repeat myself here, except to say that if you're going to feed birds using bird feeders, please do it responsibly. Start modestly with a single feeder—a tube or hopper feeder, perhaps, filled with black-oil sunflower seed—and expand your offerings from there. Try to maintain a balance between what the birds want and what you're able to offer and maintain. It's great to put up 74 feeders, but sooner or later those feeders will need to be refilled, and eventually they must be thoroughly cleaned so they don't pose a health risk to the birds. This can mean a bit of work on your part. One feeder to clean and refill is not a daunting task. More than a few feeders gets to feel a bit oppressive. Remember, this is supposed to be fun, people!

WATER

You can attract certain birds to your yard with bird feeders, but you can attract a much richer variety of birds to your yard with water. All birds need water for drinking, and most need water for bathing too. On a blistering hot August day, the water feature in the shade of our birch trees is as busy as the mall on Black Friday, while our feeders get just a few goldfinches and a half-awake chickadee or two. One look at our lists of birds that have visited our feeders and water features, and you can see how universally attractive water is to birds: feeders checklist, 49 species; water-features checklist, 70. What's more, our water offerings have attracted 23 species of warblers, often providing us with extra fine looks at these small, fast-moving, hard-to-see songbirds.

It's easy to add water to your backyard, garden, or even the deck of your condominium. If you've got a yard, the traditional birdbath on a pedestal might seem like a good choice, but I'd like you to reconsider that. There are three basic problems with pedestal birdbaths: the surface of the basin is often too slippery; the water is too high

A MALE indigo bunting and three American goldfinches visit a birdbath with recirculating water.

above the ground; and the basin, if filled up, is too deep for birds to use safely.

Pedestal birdbaths look great in the garden or backyard, and therein lies the problem: they look good to us as landscape additions, but they are usually not functional for birds to use. If they are ceramic, they are likely finished with a glaze that is slippery when wet. So any bird landing in the water will feel its feet slip and will not feel safe bathing. The same too-slick problem exists for many cheap plastic birdbaths. If birds can't get a firm footing, they won't feel safe bathing.

NATURAL-LOOKING WATER features are attractive to birds such as this Carolina chickadee.

Why? Because wet feathers make flying very difficult. If a predator surprises a bird that's just taken a soaking dip in a birdbath, the bird might not be able to evade the attack by bursting into flight. This is why songbirds approach water very cautiously.

If you already own a pedestal birdbath, take it off the pedestal and place it on the ground. Ideally, you can place it in the shade to keep the water cool and to reduce evaporation on hot days. Put a layer of pea gravel or some large flat stones in the bottom of the basin and fill it with water until the maximum depth is about 2 inches. This will make your birdbath perfectly bird-friendly.

The most important aspect of any birdbath or water feature is moving water. Moving water catches the eyes and ears of passing birds and stimulates them to bathe or drink. There are many ways to add motion to your birdbath. The easiest (and cheapest) is to fill a plastic milk jug with water, suspend it by the handle above your birdbath basin, and pierce the jug with a pin on the bottom to permit a slow drip of water to escape. You can regulate the drip rate of the water by loosening or tightening the jug's cap. This does not look wonderful (if your house is on the garden tour this summer, you might want to invest in something more aesthetically pleasing). There are a handful of small, battery-powered devices that sit in the center of your birdbath and make ripples in the water (one is called the Water Wiggler). A mister or dripper (costing about $25) will attach to your hose outlet and drip or mist the water into your bath basin. These offer relatively inexpensive ways to add motion.

With an investment of between $25 and $500, you can add a water feature with a recirculating pump to your backyard landscape. The more you spend, the more features you get, such as filters to keep the water clean, powerful, easy-to-clean pump elements, and heaters to keep the water open in winter. Our favorite has an 8-gallon reservoir with a broad shallow bath basin made from composite materials. The internal pump moves the water vertically through a hole in an artificial rock. From there the water burbles over into the wide basin and onto some smooth stones we've placed in the basin. From the first day we put this water feature out in spring until we remove it in early winter, there are birds waiting for their turn to bathe and drink.

A SHALLOW, moving source of water is most attractive to birds.

If you're feeling truly handy and ambitious, you can build your own in-ground water feature. I've seen some amazing homemade "creeks" in backyards and gardens, where water flows over 5 to 50 feet of river stones and wetland plants and into a concealed basin where it is filtered and pumped back to the top of the "creek." Such water features are sold as kits in landscaping stores and garden centers, as well as online. Some require a bit of elbow grease and engineering, so if you're not sure about your ability to build one, hire a professional to do the installation.

Four important factors to remember about water features:

1. PLACE YOUR WATER FEATURE WHERE BOTH YOU AND THE BIRDS CAN ENJOY IT. For you, this means a location where you can see the activity the feature attracts. For the birds, this means a spot that is shady, with cover nearby but not immediately adjacent (where a lurking cat could hide).

2. CLEAN THE WATER FEATURE REGULARLY. We use an abrasive sink cleaner and a scrub brush, followed by a thorough rinsing to get rid of the green scum that forms as a result of dirt, plant matter, and—let's face it—bird poop that gets into the water.

3. IF YOUR WATER FEATURE USES ELECTRICITY, be sure to use outdoor-rated electrical cords and an outlet that has a ground fault circuit interrupter to avoid an unpleasant or even harmful shock.

4. IN WINTER, if you do not plan to use a birdbath heater to keep the water open, empty your bath and bring it inside. Nothing breaks a birdbath faster than freezing in cold weather.

SHELTER

"Daddy, where do the birds go at night to sleep? Do they all have houses?" This was a question that my son, Liam, asked me when he was about six years old. It's a good question, too. The answer is that most birds seek some sort of protective shelter at night and during periods of bad weather. As the term "cavity nesters" suggests, cavity-nesting birds, such as woodpeckers, nuthatches, chickadees, titmice, bluebirds, purple martins, and some swallows, use enclosed spaces such as an old woodpecker hole or a nest box for roosting and nesting. Non–cavity-nesting birds roost in the thickest habitat they can find, offering them protection from wind, rain, and snow, as well as the searching eyes of predators. Research has shown that a well-chosen roost site in a vine tangle, pine bough, or other thick vegetation will have an ambient temperature several degrees warmer than the temperature outside the roost spot.

EVERGREENS PROVIDE nesting and roosting shelter for birds.

Some birds take this further by roosting communally and sharing body heat during the coldest nights. Bluebirds, nuthatches, and creepers have been observed crowding multiple individuals into a single tree cavity or nest box to roost together on a winter night. But even birds that do not roost in cavities, such as mourning doves and red-winged blackbirds, may crowd together at night to share body heat.

Walking the trails at dusk through the old orchard on my farm, I often unintentionally spook birds from their nighttime roosts. The cardinals, sparrows, and mourning doves that I disturb always seem to emerge from the thickest tangles of brambles and vines—in fact I almost never see them before they burst into flight, scolding me with *chip* notes (or more likely cursing me) as they go. When one of us lets our dog out late at night in the fall or winter, the activity regularly spooks a few juncos out of the cluster of arbor vitae shrubs that protect the windward side of our house. We always leave the outside light on for a while afterward to help the little snowbirds find their way back to roost.

So what can you do to provide safe and protective roosting habitat for birds? We'll answer this question with some specific suggestions in Chapter 2, but here are some concepts to get you thinking. First, look at what your yard or garden currently offers in the way of shelter for roosting birds. Are there areas of thick shrubs or viny tangles? Is there a row of pines or other conifers? Is there a fencerow or hedgerow that might serve as shelter at night or during inclement weather? Any dead trees or snags with woodpecker holes or natural cavities in them? Is there a woody edge or an area of tall grass and weeds on your property? Do you have nest boxes up around your yard? Any of these elements could serve as excellent roosting sites for your backyard birds.

A PLACE TO NEST

Many of the same habitat features that birds use for roosting can also be used as nesting sites. For birds such as gray catbirds, northern cardinals, song sparrows, and thrashers, a nice impenetrable tangle of vines, branches, thorns, and leaves is the ideal place to weave a cuplike nest of grasses, twigs, and other materials. A huge variety of birds use the year-round cover of evergreens as nesting and roosting sites. In our pines along the meadow lane, we've had everything from pine warblers to sharp-shinned hawks nesting. The big-tooth aspens along the western ridge of our farm are a

VINE TANGLES require little effort from a bird gardener, but they provide excellent bird habitat.

favorite of cavity nesters since the trees' soft wood is easy to excavate, even for chickadees and titmice. Three years ago I discovered a male pileated woodpecker excavating a nesting hole in a giant old big-tooth aspen. What a thrill it was to watch the nest throughout the spring and summer until two youngsters fledged. Soon after, a huge storm blew through our county and the nest tree split in half at the pileateds' nest hole. We were so thankful this occurred after fledging day.

On our farm we find the locations of most of the songbird nests in the late fall and winter, when the leaves are off the trees and we can see the dark shapes of last season's nests in the bare branches. It's a challenging game to try to identify the nest to the species that made it. Some are easier than others. For example, American robin nests always have grass and mud in them. Baltimore oriole nests are baglike structures that droop down from the end of a long branch, often above a roadway or stream. There are several field guides available to help you identify birds' nests. See the Resources section of this book for some suggested titles.

Almost anyone with the desire to provide housing for birds can do so in the form of nest boxes or nesting shelves. Even if you live in a condominium with no yard of your own, you can still put up a birdhouse or nesting shelf that might catch the eye of a passing house, Carolina, or Bewick's wren, or an eastern or Say's phoebe, or an American robin. I'll delve into this in greater detail in Chapter 3 when we discuss birdhouses and how to provide them properly. In short, you need to offer housing that is good for the birds, and not just aesthetically pleasing to you. Many beginners or folks who just want to add a birdhouse to their landscape design choose one for the way it looks without realizing that birds have very specific needs. It's a question of choosing function over form. Don't worry, I'll give you all the details.

Why Welcome Birds?

At this point, it's completely understandable that you might be saying to yourself "What have I gotten myself into? I just want to watch the birds. I don't want to do a million other things — I'm already busy enough!"

Like I said — perfectly understandable. And just sitting around with a mint julep in your hand, gazing sleepily at the tiny, feathered things flitting around your yard is a fine way to enjoy your backyard nature. And yet, I feel compelled to evangelize just a wee bit here on the benefits of enhancing your yard and garden. You don't have to do that much to attract many more birds.

And while we're asking ourselves the big questions, here, let's ask this one: why should you want to attract more birds to your yard or garden? They might eat all of your heirloom tomatoes, they might poop on your Porsche, and they might go all Hitchcock on the kids and pets.

I can't promise that the birds you attract aren't going to nibble on your garden veggies. Nor can I guarantee that a splotch or two of bird droppings won't appear on your car (even if it is a Porsche). I can say that you won't feel like an extra in *The Birds,* getting attacked by thousands of screaming gulls. You might get a tap on the head from an angry northern mockingbird if one nests in your yard, but let's not worry about that now, shall we?

What I can promise you is this: if you follow the tips and suggestions in this book, you will get more birds to visit your yard. Birds will enliven even the dreariest of days with their colorful plumage, their delightfully musical songs, their fascinating behavior, their amazing mastery of flight, and survival skills that make all reality TV shows pale by comparison. Furthermore, birds help reduce harmful and bothersome insects in your yard and garden, which naturally contributes to the happy balance of nature.

Not a bad deal in exchange for some small effort on your part, a few nibbled pea pods, and a bit of bird poop, huh?

Now, because I know you're still hungry for more knowledge, and because everyone likes Top Ten lists . . .

TOP TEN THINGS THAT MAKE A BIRD-FRIENDLY YARD

1. THINK IN LAYERS. Think ground level to treetops when creating your bird-friendly habitat. Start with grasses and ground covers, then perennial and annual garden plants, then shrubs, then vines, then small trees, then large trees. As in nature, a multifaceted, multilayered habitat does the best job of supplying food, shelter, and nesting space for the widest variety of species.

WHEN CREATING bird-friendly habitat, it is helpful to think in layers, from ground covers and grasses up to fully grown trees.

2. COVER THE FOUR BASICS. As mentioned earlier in this chapter, birds need food, water, shelter, and a place to nest and raise young.

3. KEEP IT HEALTHY. Don't use lawn and garden chemicals, but if you must, do so sparingly and during seasons when birds will not be exposed to them. Or use natural alternatives. The birds will thank you.

4. KEEP IT CLEAN. Clean bird feeders, water features, and nest boxes are a vital part of a healthy backyard. Avian diseases can spread at these heavily used features, so perform regular maintenance and cleaning on whatever you offer to the birds. Washing and scrubbing with a solution of 9 parts water to 1 part chlorine bleach will kill any pathogens and bacteria. Do this a few times a year on heavily used feeders, more often on water features, and once a year on nest boxes, and you'll help keep your birds healthy.

5. KEEP IT SAFE. Roaming cats, marauding hawks, raccoons and other bird-eating mammals, snakes, large glass windows— all of these things and many others kill wild birds. You can mitigate some of the impact on the birds by keeping your cats indoors (and encouraging your neighbors to do the same). Offer brush piles and other thick protective habitat for birds to use when hawks are hunting in your yard. Baffle your nest boxes to prevent mammals and snakes from climbing up mounting poles (details in Chapter 3). Place mesh netting over windows that cause a lot of bird strikes, and move feeders away from problem windows.

6. DON'T BE TOO TIDY. A tidy, perfect yard with manicured grass and a few scattered, lonely trees is not very bird-friendly. Let the edges of your yard go weedy. Encourage vines to cover an old fencerow. Leave an old dead tree standing (if human safety is not at risk), or if you must cut it down, leave some of the cut wood to form a loose wood or brush pile. Let one area of your yard stay unraked in fall and winter, so robins, thrashers, towhees, and sparrows can scratch through the leaf litter for

A WHITE-BREASTED nut hatch visits a newly filled peanut feeder.

food. All of these elements of a "messy" yard add to its bird friendliness.

7. USE THE RIGHT FEEDERS AND THE RIGHT FOODS. When you begin your bird-feeding program, make sure you're offering the right seed, and offer that seed in the appropriate feeder for the seed and the bird. Putting mixed seed in a tube feeder is an example of using the wrong feeder for the food, and the wrong food for the birds that use tube feeders. Scatter mixed seed on the ground or on a platform feeder. Use a tube feeder to offer sunflower seed, sunflower hearts, Nyjer seed, safflower, or peanuts.

8. USE PROPER HOUSING IN THE PROPER PLACES. Bluebirds cannot nest in a wren house, with its tiny entry hole. Wrens won't nest in a house that's not near some sort of cover or woodland edge. Woodpeckers prefer to excavate something from any nest box they use. Purple martins are very picky about their housing; they prefer numerous, white-colored housing units, mounted higher than any surrounding objects but in close proximity to human habitation. Starlings and house sparrows can destroy the nests of our native songbirds if we let them gain access. We'll revisit these issues in Chapter 3.

9. PLAN FOR BAD WEATHER. Make plans to be ready when bad weather hits. For sudden winter ice storms or heavy snowfall, I make a lean-to from some cinder blocks and a large heavy piece of plywood. I place this next to our brush pile, creating a small feeding zone that is out of the wind and is free of snow and ice. We also put putty-type weather stripping in the vents of our nest boxes in late fall to make the insides a bit less drafty for roosting birds. And of course when winter comes, we are stocked up with seed and high-energy foods such as peanuts, suet, and suet dough. Suet dough is a mixture of lard, peanut butter, corn meal, rolled or quick oats, and flour that is readily eaten by birds. It's a homemade alternative to raw suet or prepackaged suet cubes.

10. WATCH WHAT WORKS, LEARN FROM MISTAKES, AND MAKE IMPROVEMENTS. Remember that phrase from car commercials, "Your mileage may vary"? Well, not everything that I suggest in this book is going to work perfectly in your yard for your birds. Watch how the birds use your landscape elements. See which plants they prefer for shelter, for nesting, for food. Notice which nest boxes give birds the best success and which feeders are the busiest. This is how you will know what to do to make your yard even more bird-friendly.

TEN THINGS THAT WILL ENHANCE YOUR ENJOYMENT OF YOUR BIRD-FRIENDLY YARD

1. DON'T BE CHEAP. When purchasing things for your backyard, buy the best that you can afford. A cheap bird feeder may seem like a great deal at the store, but if the first big wind storm of the winter destroys it, you have to go buy another feeder. The same goes for binoculars, seed, nest boxes, water features, plants, and much more—buy the best you can afford. Buy quality products from a reputable retailer and you won't have to second-guess yourself later. Specialty bird stores tend to

offer higher-quality products and more expert advice than large discount stores.

2. **PLACE FEEDERS WHERE YOU CAN ENJOY THEM.** It's important that you site your feeding station and other backyard features where you can see and enjoy them from inside your home, or from your favorite place to sit outside. If you can't see your feeders, you'll never get to enjoy the fruits of your labor.

3. **USE BINOCULARS AND A FIELD GUIDE.** Lots of my nonbirding friends tell me "Oh, I just like watching the birds in my backyard, I don't really need to know what they are!" Then they proceed to ask me a bunch of bird identification questions. If you don't already have them, buy yourself a pair of starter binoculars (about $100) and a field guide to birds (about $15) and try to put a few proper names on some of your feeder visitors. Trust me: it makes backyard bird watching even more enjoyable.

4. **KEEP LISTS AND A BIRD CALENDAR.** Once you've figured out what the birds are in your yard, consider taking a few notes of interesting observations. We keep a bird calendar for arrival and departure dates of migrant birds: the first ruby-throated hummingbird in spring, the first dark-eyed junco in fall. We also note dates when other neat things happen, such as fledging day for the bluebirds in our side yard, or how many broad-winged hawks migrated over on a warm September afternoon. There are even organizations that collect such observations for their bird information databases (see the Resources section of this book for details).

5. **TAKE PICTURES OR DRAW FIELD SKETCHES.** Pocket point-and-shoot digital cameras are so great these days that you can actually take decent bird photographs with them. Thousands of people share their backyard images online on photo-sharing sites such as Flickr, on their blogs, and via social media (Twitter, Facebook, etc.). Even if you don't know the identity of the birds you photograph, someone online will be happy to help you identify them. If digital photography is not your bag, then consider drawing or sketching the birds you see. This is

IT'S A good idea to keep your binoculars and a field guide near the window that provides your best bird watching.

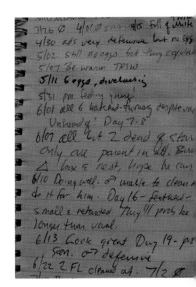

KEEPING NATURE notes about the birds, plants, and wildlife in your yard is an excellent way to learn about the seasonal occurrence and abundance of nature.

a wonderful way to become more familiar with birds, because drawing them forces you to observe them closely. I sometimes do this, though I'd never in a million years share any of my sketches. This is one of the hazards of being married to a professional artist.

6. MAKE NOTES ON WHAT THE BIRDS REALLY LIKE IN YOUR HABITAT. It's also a good idea to keep track of what's working and not working in your backyard. Feeder gets no visitors? Perhaps it's clogged or worn out. Nest box never has any successful fledglings? Perhaps it's time to install a predator baffle or move the box. We noted that the first birches and willows we planted attracted birds almost immediately. When making selections from the garden catalog in January, we referred to our notes so we knew exactly what we'd ordered and where we got it.

7. TRY SOMETHING NEW. As you become more experienced as a backyard nature lover, you'll want to try something new. I hope this book will give you plenty of ideas. There are many sources of excellent ideas at the specialty bird store, at your local library, and online. Some of the new things we've tried over the years include offering crushed eggshells to birds on the garage roof, digging a dust bath for turkeys and grouse at the edge of the yard, and offering alpaca fiber during the nest-building season. The possibilities are endless.

8. ADD A WATER FEATURE. Earlier in this chapter we talked about the importance of water for birds. If you have a birdbath, add motion to it with a wiggler, mister, or dripper. If you want to invest a bit more, buy a recirculating birdbath with a filter and a large reservoir. Moving water drives birds nuts—they cannot resist it.

9. PUT UP NEST BOXES AND MONITOR THEM. Putting up nest boxes is easy. Monitoring them requires a little more attention and effort on your part, but the rewards are worth it. In Chapters 3 and 5, I discuss nest-box monitoring in great detail. The insights and intimate connection that nest-box monitoring provides are truly special.

ADDING A water feature will attract more birds to your yard.

10. SIT QUIETLY AND ENJOY! When you've done all the planning, building, and augmenting to make your yard as bird-friendly as it can be, I have one more assignment for you: sit down and enjoy it! When my dad and I finished a handyman project, he always made a point to sit back and admire the accomplishment. That made me appreciate how a bit of focus and work can not only accomplish something, but it can give us a sense of pride in a job well done. I've never forgotten that lesson. Which is why I force my entire family to sit and appreciate things I do, like filling the bird feeders and building a brush pile.

Chapter 2: Natural Homes

ALL BIRDS NEED A "HOME"—a place to nest and to roost and rest. Ideally, this home, whether it's in the form of a nest box that we provide or simply habitat that offers sufficient shelter and cover, protects wild birds from weather, predators, and other dangers they face.

There are approximately 650 bird species that regularly nest in North America, yet fewer than 90 species (or about 13 percent) are cavity nesters—birds that nest inside a cavity, such as a hollow part of tree, an excavated hole, a nest box, a rocky crevice, or some other enclosed space. Among our passerines (perching birds), more than 75 percent build open nests (nests that are not inside cavities and lack a roof).

Primary cavity nesters are birds that create their own cavities, such as the members of the woodpecker family, which excavate a new nesting hole for each breeding attempt. Woodpeckers often also excavate roosting holes for use during the nonbreeding season. Both nesting and roosting cavities are normally used by their creators for just one season, after which they are almost certain to be used by secondary cavity nesters—birds such as chickadees, titmice, flycatchers, bluebirds, wrens, and nuthatches.

AN ADULT male pileated woodpecker feeds two hungry nestlings in a poplar snag.

Secondary cavity nesters are birds that are unable to excavate their own cavities. While a chickadee, titmouse, or nuthatch might excavate a nest cavity in extremely soft wood, it is far more usual for them to find a natural cavity in a tree, an old woodpecker hole, or a human-provided nest box to use for nesting.

Non-cavity Nesters

Most of your backyard nesters will never use a birdhouse or nest box. Here's what they do need, though: viable habitat for nesting that will permit them to reproduce successfully. For many of the bird species that are potential nesters in your yard or garden, "viable habitat" means dense vegetation where the nest and its contents are protected from extremes of weather and from the prying eyes of hungry predators. But how do you provide this in your backyard?

The answer lies in nature. Look at any piece of natural habitat in the part of the world where you reside. I'm not talking about the manicured lawn at the city park or the minimalist landscaping that surrounds most business parks. I'm talking about places where nature (not humans) is in control. What do you see? Dozens of different plant species, from ground covers and grasses to shrubs and thickets, all the way up to tall trees, growing in a naturally random way. Or if you live in an arid zone of North America, perhaps yuccas and mesquites are the shrubs, and in place of tall trees you have saguaro cacti. No matter where you live, when nature is allowed to find its own course, it forms a network of plants that are naturally useful to birds for nesting.

Birds have evolved over the eons to conceal and protect their nests from harm. Take the song sparrow, for example: It builds its nest in the thickest part of a low shrub, or it may weave it into thick grass, just above the ground. The nest is built from grasses, rootlets, and leaves, so it blends in perfectly with the surroundings. When the female song sparrow is sitting tight on the nest incubating eggs or brooding young, only the most discerning eye can pick her out from the thick, jumbled, natural setting.

A KILLDEER nest on the ground. Eggs and even the young are perfectly colored to blend in with rocky soil.

The killdeer, by contrast, builds no nest at all. It lays its eggs right on the ground, often in a shallow scrape along a road edge, railroad embankment, or gravel driveway, where the surrounding stones match the speckled earth-tone colors of its three to five eggs. The natural camouflage of the eggs, the cagey behavior of the adult killdeer, and the fact that young killdeer are able to walk away from the nest within a day of hatching all serve to mitigate the fact that the killdeer incubates its eggs on open ground.

In between these two extremes are dozens of bird species that might potentially nest in your yard or garden. As I mentioned earlier (and in the two previous books in this series), habitat variety is as important as which individual plants you choose to feature in your yard. Offering plants in a variety of sizes and seasonal fruiting, leafing, and growth patterns will make your habitat more like what occurs in nature. It will also get your patch of the world off to an excellent start to being as bird-friendly as possible.

Improving Your Yard's Nesting Potential

Aside from choosing bird-friendly plants (preferably native plants well suited to your growing zone) for your backyard habitat, there are some other things you can do to enhance your yard's nesting potential and attractiveness to birds. Some of these are the very definition of obvious, whereas others may surprise you.

TEN FEATURES TO MAKE YOUR YARD MORE ATTRACTIVE TO NESTING BIRDS

1. SPIDER WEBS. What is as stretchy as a rubber band, as strong as a steel cable, and as impact-resistant as a Kevlar bulletproof vest? Spider silk. Hummingbirds use a lot of spider silk in their tiny nests, but so do many other birds—birds in more than 20 different families, in fact. Remember this when you're cleaning up under the deck or beneath the garage eaves, and leave a few old spider webs for birds to use as nesting material.

2. DEAD GARDEN PLANTS AND WEEDS. In early spring, we often see birds stripping pieces of fine, dried plant matter off last year's winter-killed flower stalks. Many songbirds use this material in the foundation of their nests.

3. CUT GRASS. I'd be hard-pressed to name all the bird species I've seen gathering up our lawn clippings a day or so after we've mowed. This gives the grass clippings enough time to dry out and be easily gathered, transported, and worked into place. Resist the urge to rake up all the clippings when you mow, and you'll see what I mean.

4. UNRAKED LEAVES. The same holds true for leaves—they can be great nesting material in addition to providing excellent foraging opportunities for ground-feeding birds such as sparrows, towhees, thrashers, thrushes, and game birds.

5. MOSS. Many gardeners and lawn-care mavens consider moss to be a weed. Chickadees, wrens, titmice, robins, flycatchers, warblers, vireos, waxwings, hummingbirds, and scores of other birds view moss as useful nesting material. If you have a damp, mossy patch in your yard, leave it for the birds.

MANY BIRDS—especially hummingbirds—use silk from spider webs for nest building.

NESTLING CAROLINA *wrens in their nest.*

6. MUD PUDDLES. Like moss, mud is very popular as a nest-building material—the avian equivalent of mortar to a human bricklayer. Swallows in particular seem to use mud as a primary nesting material. One look at the nest of a robin, or of a barn or cliff swallow, will show you how important mud is to their nesting success.

7. DEAD TWIGS. Thrashers, catbirds, cuckoos, house and cactus wrens, and even many of our raptors are among the birds that use sticks to build their nests. I've tested the attractiveness of this material by breaking up the fine twigs of a dead branch and placing them in a loose pile along the edge of our yard in early spring—a time when I knew many of our songbirds were building their nests. I observed a northern cardinal, a house wren, and a brown thrasher poke through the sticks before selecting one each to take away to their nest site. I've also seen chimney swifts hover long enough to snap small twigs off the tops of trees for building their stick-and-saliva nests in a nearby chimney.

BIRDS USE *bare tree branches for perching when hunting, watching for danger, and as song perches. A strategically placed snag can make your yard immediately more appealing to birds.*

8. DEAD TREES. Among the most attractive features of any bird-friendly yard is a large dead tree. Your local landscape designer might disagree, and your insurance agent might want you to remove all dead wood that could fall and damage anyone or anything, but the birds will thank you in every way they know how. Believe it or not, a large dead tree might hold more active nests than its still-alive neighbor of the same species. Woodpeckers, being primary cavity nesters, love nothing more than a nice dead snag in which to drill a nest or roost hole. After they are done using these cavities, other species will use them too. It's not uncommon to see a large dead snag that has the remains of a raptor nest built in its upper branches, a woodpecker nest drilled and active in its trunk, and perhaps a bluebird or swallow nest in an old woodpecker hole, or a flycatcher nest in a natural knothole. If you can safely keep a dead tree or add a dead snag to your yard, do it!

9. PET OR HUMAN HAIR. My barber used to think it was weird when I asked to keep the (salt-and-pepper-colored) hair clippings from my haircuts. Now he asks me if I want them. I scatter them in clumps around the yard, along with daughter Phoebe's red hair, son Liam's blond hair, and wife Julie's (not as graying as mine) hair. We've found nearly a dozen different nests over the years with our hair in the lining. This works well with pet hair too; chipping and song sparrows love to line their nests with animal hair.

Once I was asleep in my hammock on the patio under the back deck when I was awakened by a painful tug on the side of my head. A tufted titmouse had shifted its attention from the ball of hair clippings on the deck above, to get some more nesting material right from the source. I guess it wanted to cut out the middle man!

10. EGGSHELLS. Egg production by female birds drains a lot of calcium from their bodies. Eggshells are an excellent way for these birds to restore healthy levels of calcium. Eggshell bits also serve as grit to help insect- and seed-eating birds such as swallows, flycatchers, and goldfinches break up hard-shelled food items. Save your eggshells after you whip up a delicious breakfast, rinse them out, and bake them in a pan in the oven at 250 degrees for 10 minutes to kill off any disease agents present in the eggs. Crush them in a large jar (we use a wooden spoon) and spread them out on bare ground, a deck railing, platform

BARN SWALLOWS are fond of crushed eggshells, particularly during the nesting season.

feeder, or other spot where passing birds can see the white shell bits. Nesting birds will benefit greatly from this unusual offering.

How to Spot Nesting Birds

Now that we've discussed how to make your yard more appealing to nesting birds, I am absolutely certain you'll be the landlord to a few more tenants. How will you know this for sure? You'll act just like a detective trying to solve a mystery: you'll look for clues. Here are some leads.

DETERMINE WHEN THE NESTING SEASON IS FOR YOUR PART OF THE WORLD

Although some birds, such as the mourning dove, are known to nest in any month of the year, most of our backyard birds nest during the warmer, food-rich seasons of spring and summer. In southernmost North America, spring can mean January. In the far, far north, spring and summer combined may last only a few weeks. A few bird species stretch the season earlier and later. For example, the American goldfinch waits to nest until August when the thistle down it lines its nests with is readily available. The great horned owl on our farm is already feeding young owlets in the nest in February. But I know that here on our farm the bulk of songbird nesting happens from mid-April through mid-July, with May and June as the peak months.

Consult local bird-watching experts, the folks at your specialty bird-feeding store, or your state or provincial breeding bird atlas to determine the peak months of the year for nesting birds. This will help you determine when to be ready to be a good landlord, and when to begin looking for clues of nesting activity.

A MALE indigo bunting sings from a favorite song perch in a tulip poplar tree.

LOOK AND LISTEN FOR COURTSHIP

The spring nesting season starts with male birds setting up territories and courting potential mates. Resident birds (species that do not migrate away from their year-round territories) will begin spring singing as soon as they feel the urge. I've heard northern cardinals, song sparrows, Carolina chickadees, and other resident birds here on our farm singing their full spring songs on sunny days in late January. Birds are highly sensitive to the increasing day length of late winter, which increases their production of sex hormones, stimulating singing. Migrant species (birds that migrate to warmer climes in the fall, spend the winter there, and return in the spring) usually begin spring courtship a bit later. Males return first in an attempt to grab the best territories. Once they find a suitable spot, they begin to set up their turf, singing to attract the attention of passing females, and to warn passing rival males not to trespass.

As the resident birds tune up to full spring voice, they are joined in song by the returning migrants—and spring mornings become a riot of bird song and activity. Birds from last year's nesting season that have survived the rigors of winter or migration are ready to find a mate and breed. A first-year adult male Baltimore oriole, for example, may return to the black willow tree in Tennessee where it was hatched last summer only to find itself driven away by its own father, who still retains title to this prime nesting site. Even if most songbirds don't recognize their relatives the way we humans do, a territorial adult male certainly sees another adult male of its species as a potential rival.

Side note: Most songbirds do not even recognize themselves, which is why birds confronted with their reflected image in a car mirror or pane of clean window glass will fight their reflection as though it is a rival.

WATCH FOR TERRITORIAL FIGHTING

The return of females ups the ante in your yard. Now males must go all out to win a mate and vanquish all challengers. This is the season of loud singing, wing waving, and courtship demonstrations, of high-speed chases and tumbling, and of pitched battles between rival males and often females, too. If you have a bird in your backyard or garden that is a regular singer from a regular perch—say, a male spotted towhee—notice where and when he does his singing. All territorial male songbirds have a series of song perches, which they use in rotation to cover their territories. You can get a reasonable idea of the size and shape of your towhee's territory by watching and plotting from where he broadcasts his songs.

IS HE COURTSHIP FEEDING?

After you observe the courtship and get an idea of your towhee's territory, you should see some evidence that the male was successful in attracting a mate (if indeed he was). The female spotted towhee is a drab-colored version of her mate, which makes her more difficult to detect when she's on the nest. If the male has attracted a mate, you may see him bring her food items and feed them to her. This is called "courtship feeding," and it serves to strengthen the pair bond as well as strengthen the female for the challenges she faces in nest building, egg laying, and brood rearing. Northern cardinals are common backyard birds that are famous for their courtship feeding behavior, sometimes called the "cardinal kiss."

LOOK FOR NESTS

You may or may not see your female towhee as she comes and goes during nest building. The nest site will be a scrape on the ground filled with a woven cup of grasses, rootlets, twigs, and bark strips, lined with animal hair. She will diligently gather the nesting materials and weave them into the nest, forming the cup shape using her belly and bill. As a female robin builds a nest, she will make regular trips to your lawn to gather dry grass and to a nearby puddle for mud, returning each time to the nest site. Robins nest in a wide variety of situations, from easy-to-find sites such as on the eave of a building or the top of an outdoor light fixture, to more hidden places such as deep in a shrub.

Woodpecker nests are among the easiest to locate. The noise of excavation as the cavity is being formed by repeated hacking of the bill on wood is a great early season clue. The finished cavity is often obvious—basically a dark hole on a tree trunk, usually under an overhanging limb. Anytime you see a bird—male or female—with an item that is clearly not food, it is likely to be nesting material. If you watch such a scene patiently, the bird may reveal the approximate location of the nest as it carries the material to the site.

WATCH FOR COPULATION

During spring and summer, as the nesting season for most birds swings into action, you may have the chance to observe birds copulating. Copulation between male and female songbirds is brief, often occurring on the ground or on a stable perch. In very general terms, a typical copulation between a male and female songbird goes like this: The male approaches the female closely, perhaps vibrating his wings excitedly. He may utter short song phrases or a series of chips or notes. If she is receptive to his advances, she may call back and shake her wings, and turn to present her back to the male. He will mount her back, and they will shift slightly back and forth so that his cloaca and hers are in contact.

A single copulation, lasting only a few seconds, is enough to fertilize an entire clutch of eggs for most songbirds. Despite this possibility, many of our songbirds, such as tree swallows, can be seen copulating

TREE SWALLOWS copulate.

many times daily. After copulation, the female continues or finishes nest building so she'll have a place to lay the eggs forming inside her.

LOOK FOR EGGS

Once the nest is built, the female towhee, like most other songbirds, will lay one egg per day, just after dawn, until the clutch is completed (usually two to six eggs for spotted towhees). After she lays the last egg, she'll begin incubating. During the incubation and nestling stages, most songbird pairs will become quiet and very secretive. The male may still perform territorial songs at dawn and even throughout the day, but once there are hungry nestlings to be fed and protected, his singing tapers off and his energy is devoted to these tasks.

LISTEN FOR NOISY NESTLINGS

Birds come into this world, hatching out of eggs, in one of two forms: precocial or altricial. Precocial means a hatchling emerges from the egg covered in down, eyes open, and able to move around on its own shortly after hatching. A good example of a precocial bird is the killdeer, a shorebird that commonly nests on gravel-covered ground, often near human habitation. Hatchling killdeer emerge from the egg and within an hour begin walking around, following their parents and mimicking their foraging behavior.

TWO RECENTLY fledged northern parulas just after leaving the nest.

Altricial birds are born naked (initially lacking down), with eyes closed and completely helpless. Altricial nestlings must be cared for by a parent for a period of days to several weeks, until they develop sufficiently to fledge from the nest. The birds classified as passerines, which include all of our common backyard songbirds, have altricial young.

For the first days after hatching, altricial nestlings are stimulated to open their bill to beg for food by the sound and vibration of an adult returning to the nest with food. As they grow, the nestlings become more vocal, and if you happen to be near the nest you may hear the high-pitched peeping of these hungry tots.

SOME LANDLORDS keep track of their nest-box tenants by watching from a distance, which allows the nesting birds to come and go without fear.

KEEP AN EYE OUT FOR SECRETIVE, DEFENSIVE PARENTS

For their part, the parents will be very secretive and skulking now that they have a nest full of youngsters to tend. Every trip to and from the nest is taken with great caution. Watch for the adults, pausing with a bill full of food as they survey their surroundings before heading to the nest, often via a roundabout path designed to conceal their true destination. This is also the time when anyone approaching the nest area, human or predator, may be met with harsh, loud scolding notes and, in some cases, direct physical challenges by the adults. Northern mockingbirds are well known for their aggressive defense of their nest zone, driving off dogs, cats, hawks, and humans with missile-like attack flights right at the trespasser's head.

WATCH CAREFULLY FROM A DISTANCE

If you're a good detective and spend some time "staking out" your backyard nesting birds' behavior, you'll probably learn the locations of several nests. This is when you need to resist the urge to move in for a closer look. All of the creatures that prey on birds, their nests, and young have learned that human scent trails often lead to food, whether it's a garbage can or compost pile, a pet-food dish or picnic table. If you visit a nest and peek inside the covering vegetation for a closer look, several bad things can happen. You have just left a scent trail that points like a giant smelly arrow directly to an easy meal of eggs or nestlings. If the nestlings are old enough to be near fledging, you may spook them from the nest early, making it harder for their parents to find and feed them and making them more vulnerable to predators. After the nesting season is done, you can go back for a peek to confirm your hunch about the nest's location.

In the next chapter we'll examine how and why visiting the nest-box nests of your cavity-nesting tenants is perfectly acceptable—even encouraged.

Facts about Birds' Nests

NEST SITE

While the stereotypical image of a bird's nest is a cup-shaped nest built in the forked branch of a tree, in reality, birds nest in all kinds of situations and settings. Following is a list of some typical nest sites used by North American birds, and some of the common birds that prefer them.

Bank: bank swallow (funny how some birds are just named right!), kingfisher

Ground: killdeer and many game birds, such as grouse and wild turkey

Cliff: cliff swallow, white-throated swift, many raptors

Shrub: many songbirds, such as northern cardinal and gray catbird

Deciduous tree: warblers, orioles, vireos

Coniferous tree: finches, some warblers, nuthatches

Snag: wood duck, many woodpeckers, tree swallow

Vine tangle: yellow-breasted chat, thrashers, some wrens

Floating on water: many ducks, geese, loons

CLIFF SWALLOWS build jug-shaped nests using mud carried to the site one billfull at a time. Each nest represents hundreds of trips.

NEST TYPE

Bird nests can be placed in the following general categories, based on how they are constructed: scrape (on the ground), cup, saucer, hammock, platform, cavity, crevice, burrow, pendent, sphere.

Here are some examples of common birds that construct each nest type.

Scrape: most shorebirds, American woodcock

Cup: American robin and many other songbirds, including flycatchers, jays, warblers

Saucer: tanagers, many doves

Hammock: chimney swift

Platform: most raptors

BALTIMORE ORIOLES build baglike nests by weaving together stems of grass and other fibers. This is a male Baltimore oriole.

Cavity: bluebirds, chickadees, titmice, woodpeckers, many owls, some ducks, some flycatchers

Crevice: white-throated swift, canyon wren, rock wren, some seabirds, such as puffins

Burrow: kingfishers, some seabirds, burrowing owl, bank swallow

Pendent: orioles, some flycatchers, kinglets

Sphere: marsh wren, sedge wren, cactus wren, great kiskadee, magpies, verdin

CONSTRUCTION

A nest must be constructed of materials that will hold, cushion, and protect the eggs and young. It also needs to stand up to parental visits and active growing nestlings. Birds are very utilitarian when it comes to the materials they use to build their nests. Some birds, like the gulls and many shorebirds, merely kick out a depression in the ground or scrape together a small amount of nesting material to protect the nest from tides and wind. More elaborate construction, such as that of many of our songbirds, involves structural material, woven or bound together by an adhesive ingredient (water, saliva, spider silk, mud, or plant fibers) and lined with a soft, sometimes insulating material such as moss or animal hair. Many of our hawk species and purple martins routinely add green leaves to their nests as a sort of natural insect repellent. And of course since birds live among us, it's no surprise that they also sometimes incorporate human-made materials (string, plastic bags, shiny objects) into their nests.

Eleven Exceptional Nest Builders

Here are descriptions of 11 common North American birds and their unique nests.

1. CLIFF SWALLOW. Cliff swallows build their gourd-shaped nests one billfull of mud at a time, adhering to a cliff face or, in modern times, to the side of a barn, bridge, or culvert. A single nest takes about two weeks to construct and involves as many as 2,100 individual trips from the mud source to the nest site. Once built, however, these nests are a safe and comfortable place to raise a family, especially since cliff swallow colonies may include as many as 1,000 nesting pairs.

2. PILEATED WOODPECKER. A few springs ago, I discovered a male pileated woodpecker excavating a nesting cavity in a big-tooth aspen on our farm. I watched the entire nesting process from inside a portable photography blind. What an amazing excavation job! A carpenter with power tools could not have created the cavity any faster. In the end, two young pileateds fledged from a cavity that was 8 to 10 inches wide and 18 inches deep. The entry hole was just wide enough for the adults to slip in and out while tending the nest.

A PILEATED woodpecker in the middle of excavation work at a nest cavity.

3. BALTIMORE ORIOLE. In North America, the orioles are the champions of pendent nest construction, and the Baltimore oriole, being a common nesting species across much of eastern North America and Canada, often places its nest on the end of a drooping branch over water or a roadway. It's made from grasses and plant fiber and lined with soft plant down or animal fur. The Baltimore oriole can complete this very complex but sturdy nest in as few as five days.

4. BLACK-CHINNED HUMMINGBIRD. All hummingbirds build amazing, tiny, stretchable nests, but the black-chinned hummingbird seems to be the most willing of the hummingbird species to nest near human habitation. Hummingbird enthusiasts in the Southwest have noticed a trend in the past decade or so of black-chinned hummingbirds nesting under the eaves of houses, in open sheds and outbuildings, and on the wire hooks of hanging plants. The main impetus for these close-to-people nests seems to be to get out of the wind, since high winds can blow tiny hummingbird eggs and nestlings right out of the nest. What a treat to have a hummingbird nest so close!

5. BROWN CREEPER. The brown creeper splits the difference between being an open-cup nester and a cavity nester. Since this species makes its living by gleaning insects and larvae from beneath the bark of trees, it's no surprise that creepers also nest beneath bark. But they do not excavate a cavity. Instead they find a large, loose piece of bark and build a hammock-like nest beneath it, against the trunk of the tree. The nest is made of small branches, bark bits, pine needles, and spider silk and is lined with moss or feathers.

6. CHIMNEY SWIFT. Chimney swifts come by their name honestly—they nest almost exclusively in chimneys (though some nest in hollow trees, caves, wells, and other chimney-like structures). The chimney swift's nest is a tiny hammock made of fine twigs glued together and to the chimney wall with the bird's sticky, clear saliva. Chimney swifts gather the twigs for the nest in flight, swooping and hovering long enough to grab a twig and snap it off the top of a tree.

7. CHICKADEES. Members of the chickadee family are clever and feisty nesters. As secondary cavity nesters they rely on old woodpecker holes, naturally occurring cavities, or nest boxes for their sites. They build their nest from mosses and soft plant material and line them with feathers and animal hair. When leaving the eggs to go foraging, the adult chickadees cover the eggs with fur to hide them from nosy neighboring birds and to keep them warm.

8. OVENBIRD. Although not a common backyard bird, the ovenbird deserves major kudos for its namesake Dutch oven–shaped nest. Built in the open on the woodland floor, the domed nest is made of leaves, branches, dried grasses, and other natural materials, helping it blend in perfectly with its surroundings. Inside, the nest is lined with animal hair, and the adults go in and out through a tiny arched opening.

9. CACTUS WREN. As its name suggests, the cactus wren is heavily associated with members of the cactus family in the desert Southwest. Cactus wrens prefer to make their globe-

BIRDS THAT build cup nests often use grasses, rootlets, and small vines in the construction.

shaped nests in cholla cactus or other thorny shrubs. The nests are bulky structures about a foot wide, made of grasses and plant stems and lined with feathers. It is believed that the prickly, thorny location of the nests helps thwart would-be nest predators.

10. KILLDEER. It's not so much the building of the killdeer's nest that warrants its inclusion on this list. After all, the killdeer nest is a mere scrape made in gravelly soil. It's the lengths to which adult killdeer will go to protect the nest. Adults will begin calling a piercing *dee-dee-dee* when danger threatens, then one or both will perform a broken-wing display, trying to lure predators away from the nest by feigning injury (and thus looking like an easy meal to a fox, raccoon, or other nest predator).

11. EASTERN PHOEBE. I always marvel at the audacious nest sites chosen by eastern phoebes. They will build their mud, grass, and moss nests on door frames, porch lights, and window sills, as well as in old buildings, under bridges, and in caves. They seem to try to select sites that are difficult for snakes to access. Alas, the nesting phoebes on our farm often lose later broods to these hungry reptiles. The return of the phoebes here in southeastern Ohio is always a sign that spring is on its way. We have a soft spot for this species, having named our first child in its honor.

CACTUS WREN nests are a ball of sticks, usually placed in some thorny location such as this one in a cholla cactus.

EASTERN PHOEBES will nest on any protected ledge. This one is nesting on a shelf under the eaves of a house.

Bird Nests: True or False?

1. The mourning dove builds one of the flimsiest nests of all North American birds.

True. Most mourning dove nests consist of a few twigs in a loose pile—barely enough to be considered a nest. The sad result is that lots of mourning dove eggs fall out of the nest before hatching.

Since this species has been observed nesting in all months of the year, it does not have the evolutionary incentive to invest a great deal of time and energy into nest building. If its nest fails, it can simply try again.

2. It's a good idea to offer long pieces of string for birds to use in their nests.
False. If you want to offer string, make sure the pieces are cut shorter than 3 inches to avoid entangling nestlings.

3. A red-bellied woodpecker will use the same nest hole year after year.
False. All woodpeckers excavate a new nest hole for each nesting attempt.

4. The material that permits hummingbird nests to expand as the nestlings grow is spider silk.
True. Female hummingbirds rely on spider silk for nest construction. This natural material helps bind the nest together so that it retains its cup shape during egg laying and incubation and also permits the nest to expand as the nestlings grow.

5. It's a good idea to try to find birds' nests whenever you can.
False. Approaching a nest built in natural habitat may disturb nestlings and tip off predators to its location. It's okay to visit nest boxes that are equipped with predator baffles.

6. Most birds are considered cavity nesters.
False. More than 85 percent of all North American nesting birds do not nest in cavities. Most are open-cup nesters.

7. Barn swallows are so named because they will nest only in barns.
False. Barn swallows will nest on any structure to which they can adhere their mud nests—culverts, cliff faces, caves, barns, etc.

8. Some birds build nests that float on the surface of the water.

CUP NESTERS such as these yellow-billed cuckoos have evolved several survival strategies. Hatchlings leave the nest just a few days after hatching, but if they're disturbed while still in the nest, they perform an impressive snakelike display designed to scare potential predators.

True. The common loon is an expert at this type of nesting structure.

9. Altricial nestlings come out of the egg already in adult plumage and ready to mate.
False. Altricial hatchlings are bald, blind, and helpless at birth. Precocial hatchlings are downy, open-eyed, and mobile at birth. Altricial young develop physically and grow their first set of feathers before leaving the nest. Precocial young leave the nest immediately, so these physical changes take place away from the nest.

10. Some birds, such as the cactus wren, intentionally build their nests in places that offer additional protection, such as the thorns on a cactus.
True. The aptly named cactus wren prefers to build its ball-of-sticks nest in the thickest, thorniest parts of cacti such as cholla. I have observed brown thrasher and yellow-breasted chat nests in the center of large rose thickets. There's no doubt that these nest sites provide added protection against predation.

Shelter: Make Your Yard a Safe Haven for Birds

This section includes a brief overview of some of the most bird-friendly plants in each of the general categories that gardeners and landscapers use. Not all of these suggestions will work in your climate and growing zone, so please use these as a starting point as you plan your backyard habitat enhancements. Local expertise with native plants is incredibly valuable when building a bird-friendly habitat.

SOME SHELTERING PLANTS FOR NESTING BIRDS

Grasses and ground covers. Ferns, goldenrod, asters, creeping thyme, marjoram, ironweed, milkweed, native prairie grasses such as buffalo grass and little bluestem, annual grasses such as red fountaingrass, and perennials such as coreopsis, zinnias, cosmos, black-eyed Susan, sunflowers.

AN EASTERN Kingbird incubates eggs in a nest atop a tree snag.

VINES SUCH as *Virginia creeper offer thick foliage as shelter and fleshy berries as a food source in autumn.*

Shrubs and hedges. Hollies, yews, boxwood, arbor vitae, cedars, pyracantha, elderberry, wax myrtle, viburnums, sumacs, forsythia.

Pricklies and sticklies. Raspberries, blackberries, hollies, native hawthorns (avoid barberries).

Small-to-medium deciduous trees with dense foliage. Dogwoods, birches, mulberries, redbud, willows, magnolias.

Large deciduous trees with dense foliage. Oaks, maples, ashes, poplars, sycamores, beech, hickory, walnut.

Conifers. Native pines, spruces, cedars, arbor vitae.

Vines. Wild grapes, native honeysuckles (such as coral honeysuckle), Virginia creeper, trumpet vine (native but highly invasive; plant this where you will mow all around it).

SHELTERING STRUCTURES

You can augment the attractiveness of your bird-friendly backyard by adding these structures that offer many backyard birds opportunities for roosting, foraging, and nesting.

Brush piles provide your feeder birds with important shelter from predators as well as from extremes of weather.

Rock walls give birds an excellent place to forage for insects, grubs, ants, and other delectables.

Wood piles are among the best overwintering sites for insects and thus offer excellent foraging for nesting birds. Our Carolina wrens pick beetle larvae and dormant insects out of our old woodpile all winter long.

Dead trees and snags can be excellent nesting sites for all primary and secondary cavity nesters. They also attract perch-and-hunt species such as flycatchers, bluebirds, shrikes, and kestrels.

Edge habitat. Where an open area such as a lawn or field meets the edge of the woods, it creates a transition zone between the two habitats. Edge habitat can be incredibly rich for birds and wildlife, especially if the transition is gradual and not abrupt (such as mowed lawn abutting canopy forest). A great number of backyard bird species prefer the brushy, messy edge zone.

Hedgerows, fencerows, and windbreaks. Modern agriculture trends have resulted in the elimination of many of these features.

Hedgerows and fencerows not only serve to mark the line between two pieces of land, but they also serve as vital habitat for wildlife, especially in open country, where a fencerow or windbreak may be the only bit of standing vegetation and shelter for miles around. Birds such as quail, pheasant, bluebirds, orioles, sparrows, flycatchers, and many others rely on these patches of thick shelter to survive.

Stumps. While your first instinct might be to remove an old tree stump, think again. Although it may not host a nesting bird, it will certainly provide foraging opportunities for woodpeckers, nuthatches, chickadees, titmice, wrens, and others that will glean, chisel, and pry at the decaying wood of the stump to get at grubs, beetles, and other creatures that live in rotting wood.

Roost boxes. Lest we forget: the nest boxes of spring and summer are the roost boxes of fall and winter. Prepare your nest boxes for winter by repainting or restaining the exterior, and place some dried, soft grasses on the inside. If you want to go further, follow our lead and use pliable weather stripping to plug the vent holes on

SOFT-WOOD TREES such as this old gray birch trunk are often full of holes from foraging woodpeckers and from chickadees and titmice excavating nest or roost holes.

HEDGEROW HABITAT offers birds shelter for roosting or nesting as well as foraging opportunities.

Chapter 3: Bird Housing

IN THIS CHAPTER we'll look at getting started as a nest-box landlord, including general considerations for selecting and placing housing. We'll also share some specific information about a few of our most common nest-box–using birds: purple martins and our three species of bluebirds.

NEST BOXES *with predator baffles enjoy vastly higher rates of nesting success since they virtually eliminate access by climbing predators.*

What Is a Birdhouse?

Birdhouse, nest box, bird box—all of these terms refer to human-supplied nesting space for birds. In the last chapter we discussed natural habitat that birds nest in—those species that do not use nest boxes or nest in cavities. In this chapter we'll examine what features make for good nest boxes, where and when to place them, and how to monitor them. In the next chapter we'll examine the bird species that regularly use human-supplied housing.

Why Do This?

Being a landlord to the birds is not for everyone. In fact, it can be a lot of work and take an investment of time, money, and energy if you want to do it right. But like the credit card commercial says, the benefits are "priceless." A unique and special connection develops between nesting birds and the people who care for them. Not only are we gifted with an intimate look inside the lives of "our" nesting birds, but we also get the satisfaction of knowing we are helping these creatures sustain their populations in the face of habitat loss, pressure from predators and nest-site competitors, weather extremes, food shortages, and lack of naturally available nesting cavities. We've been providing nest boxes for a variety of cavity-nesting species on our farm for the past 20 years, and I can tell you that the benefits far outweigh the difficulties.

Humans and birds have been coexisting for thousands of years, but it's been only in the past few hundred years that we have been supplying housing for birds to nest here in North America. Can you guess which bird species was the first one to nest in human-supplied hous-

A PURPLE *martin house with nesting martins.*

ing? No, it wasn't Archaeopteryx! It was the purple martin. And that's why in the anthem "God Bless America" it says "for purple martins' majesty . . ."

Okay, I'm stretching the truth there a bit, but purple martins were the first wild bird species in North America to take advantage of human-supplied housing.

The Purple Martin Story

The purple martin is the largest member of the swallow family in North America and the only North American swallow that we call a martin (there are many other martins in Europe and in Central and South America). Adult male purple martins are deep, glossy purple overall, though in many light conditions they appear to be black. Females and young birds are dark brown or gray with white bellies.

In the early 1800s, ornithologist Alexander Wilson observed purple martins nesting in hollowed-out gourds that Native Americans had placed around their villages. His notes about this are the first documented record of human-supplied housing being used by birds in North America. The relationship between the villagers and the martins was symbiotic: the martins got free nesting sites, and the villagers got insect control around their homes and food supplies. One added benefit to the village was that the martins would sound an alarm any time a stranger or animal approached.

The Native Americans grew the gourds they used themselves, and to this day "birdhouse gourds" are still used.

MORE MARTIN NATURAL HISTORY

Before they used gourds, purple martins nested in natural situations, such as in old woodpecker holes or in cavities on cliff faces. Over the hundreds of years that humans and purple martins have been living together, martins have become more and more reliant on human-supplied housing. In fact, in the eastern two-thirds of North America, martins nest almost exclusively in martin houses, often in large colonies of dozens or even hundreds of birds. Only in the desert Southwest and in the Pacific Northwest do purple martins still nest regularly in natural cavities.

Martins are very social birds and prefer to nest colonially. They can be pretty selective—picky, even—about where they will nest. We've had martin houses up on our farm for 20 years, and while we've

PURPLE MARTINS are colonial nesters—they prefer to nest in close proximity to other martins.

had a few young males stop by to investigate, we've never had even a single pair of martins nest here. The reason is that we lack a permanent source of water, such as a pond or lake, here on our dry ridgetop, and there is not another martin colony nearby from which to attract homesteaders. Purple martins prefer housing that is painted white, is placed within 100 feet or so of human habitation such as a house or barn, and that is the highest thing in the immediate vicinity, offering clear flying space in all directions. A nearby body of water such as a pond, lake, or river will greatly enhance the attractiveness for martins, both as a source of insects and for drinking water. If your property and housing do not meet these requirements, it's unlikely that you'll get purple martins to nest.

If what you can offer does meet these requirements, then get ready to be a purple martin landlord. Purple martins spend the spring and summer in the U.S. and Canada and the winter in South America. Each spring, martin enthusiasts anxiously await the arrival of the spring "scouts." These are adult males that return early to the colony where they were hatched in hopes of getting the prime nesting cavities for themselves. Martins are very loyal to their nesting colonies, returning year after year to breed. In the Deep South, the first scouts are reported as early as mid-January, and by May 1 the most northerly nesting martin scouts have reached their colonies—even as far north as northern Maine.

One problem these early-arriving scouts sometimes encounter is inclement weather. Purple martins eat flying insects, which they catch in flight. When the weather is cold, rainy, snowy, or icy for a few days and the insects are not flying, martins can become weak and may even starve. A handful of inventive, long-time martin landlords have come up with some interesting solutions to keep their martins fed when the weather turns bad. Because martins catch insects only while in flight, putting mealworms on a feeder does them no good—they don't naturally forage while perched. Instead, the crafty martin landlords stand under their martin colonies and use spoons to fling insects into the air. That's right! They place small crickets, soft mealworms, and even tiny pieces of scrambled egg in the cup of a spoon and fling it skyward. As soon as the martins see a "flying" insect, they are stimulated to pursue it and in this way at least some of the starving martins can be saved. Some of these same experienced landlords have managed to teach their martins to eat these same foods off platform feeders, but only after the martins have been clued in to the new food item by seeing and catching "flying" food.

STARTING YOUR MARTIN COLONY

Before you get set up to host nesting purple martins, check to see how close the nearest established colony is. New colonies are typically formed when young males from a nearby colony are forced to look elsewhere for their own nesting cavities. If you do not know of any purple martin nesting colonies within a few miles of your home, you might wish to contact one of the martin conservation organizations listed in the Resources section of this book.

Even if there is no nearby colony, it is still possible to attract martins to your new site, provided your location meets the qualities that martins seek. Here are more details about what you need to do.

A PURPLE martin decoy.

- Place housing in the center of an area that measures at least 40 square feet, with no trees near the housing.

- Locate housing within 120 feet of human habitation.

- Paint houses or gourds white.

- Make sure housing has proper interior dimensions and entry-hole size: floor dimensions should measure at least 6 x 6 inches. Internal height can be from 5 to 7 inches high. Entrance hole should be about 1 inch above the floor. Hole size can range from 1¾ inches up to 2¼ inches, but 2⅛ inches is recommended.

- Mount housing at a height between 10 and 17 feet.

- Make sure no wires lead to housing (wires can permit predators to gain access).

A few tricks that martin landlords use to lure birds to new colonies include adding life-sized decoys of adult male martins to the housing to make a new colony appear active, and playing a recording of the dawn song sung by male martins. The martins' dawn song is performed by adult males flying in the sky above an established colony, often before first light. It is meant as an audio beacon to attract passing migrant martins (especially females) to the colony. You can purchase recordings of the dawn song as well as martin decoys from martin conservation organizations.

Aspiring martin landlords can find more useful information and purchase supplies at the wonderful websites of several martin conservation organizations (listed in the Resources section of this book). Many of these sites also feature forums where landlords share ideas, experiences, advice, and solutions for better purple martin nesting success.

A FEMALE eastern bluebird.

The Bluebird Story

In the mid-1970s, members of the Audubon Naturalist Society in Chevy Chase, Maryland, began a campaign to publicize the sad plight of the eastern bluebird. The eastern bluebird was once a common and familiar bird all across rural eastern North America, but it had been experiencing a decades-long decline and was now lamentably scarce. The causes of the decline were obvious: reduced availability of nesting cavities as a result of harvesting dead trees for firewood; the shift from the use of wood to metal and concrete fenceposts and power poles; increased competition for nest cavities from European starlings and house sparrows, two non-native species; and increased use of chemicals in agriculture and lawn care. To combat this decline, a handful of bluebird enthusiasts formed the North American Bluebird Society and began promoting the cause of all three bluebird species in a grassroots outreach campaign. The effort gained steam when several national media outlets covered the plight of the bluebirds, and soon, with the increased attention, bluebird nest boxes began appearing in appropriate habitat all over North America. The bluebirds responded by using these new nest cavities, with the happy result that their populations rebounded.

THREE BLUEBIRDS

There are three bluebird species in North America: eastern bluebird, western bluebird, and mountain bluebird. All three are mostly blue, especially adult males, with females and young birds being subtler

A MALE western bluebird.

A MALE mountain bluebird.

shades of blue and gray. One or more bluebird species can be found breeding in 49 states of the U.S. and in nearly every province in Canada. Sorry, Hawaii, no bluebirds for you.

Eastern bluebird. Male eastern bluebirds are cobalt blue on the back, wings, and head, with a pale gray throat, rusty breast, and white belly. Females mimic these colors and patterns in more subtle hues.

Western bluebird. Males are similar to male easterns but have more rust on the back. The blue of male western bluebirds is a deeper, ultramarine blue. Females, though paler, also have the rusty back and breast.

Mountain bluebird. Our largest bluebird, the mountain bluebird is one of the few birds in North America that is almost all blue. Male mountains show a pale white lower belly but no rust. Females are the grayest of the female bluebirds. Mountain bluebirds nest at higher elevations in summer and migrate to lower elevations—often in large flocks—in winter.

BLUEBIRD TRAILS AND CLUBS

The human outreach to help nesting bluebirds has not only stabilized the populations of these three thrush species and helped them expand into viable habitat, but it has also resulted in the establishment of thousands of miles of bluebird trails, and clubs all across the continent. Nearly every state and province has a bluebird organization, the members of which maintain and monitor nest boxes along these bluebird trails. A bluebird trail is a series of nest boxes placed in ideal bluebird habitat that is maintained and monitored during the breeding season by a trail operator. If you've ever seen bluebird houses on a fence along a highway, around the edge of a golf course, or on the edge of a hayfield, you've seen a bluebird trail. A closer look might reveal a number on each nest box. These numbers are used to keep seasonal nesting records for each box and each nesting attempt. The data, collected by the trail operator, are invaluable in determining bluebird nesting success, population stability, and the effects of predators, weather, food shortages, pesticides, and other issues facing bluebirds.

We'll talk about setting up your own bluebird trail a bit later in this chapter.

Proper Housing for Birds

If there is one single thing I hope to convey to readers of this book (this means you!), it is how to offer the appropriate housing in the proper way to your birds. This has to do with construction, entrance-hole diameter, internal dimensions, and where and how you offer the housing. So many backyard bird products these days are either meant to be decorative and appeal to humans or are so poorly designed and cheaply made that, if they last an entire season, they won't work for birds anyway. You can buy a gorgeous Victorian-style purple martin house, hand painted to look like a mansion the Vanderbilts would have lived in (had they been tiny), with entry

DECORATIVE HOUSES, *like the two on the left, are pretty, but not as functional for birds as the less attractive nest box on the right.*

holes that are so small a chickadee couldn't get inside. Or you can buy a nest box adorned with the colors of your alma mater that has a roof that leaks. Do the birds a favor and keep both of these purchases on the mantle in the living room. If you place them outside and birds try to use them, the birds will only be frustrated (at best) or come to an unfortunate end (at worst).

A birdhouse or nest box that's made with birds in mind will have the following features:

- Be made from either natural wood (at least ¾ inch thick), ideally red or white cedar, which weathers well, or from thick, durable plastic or composite material.

- Pieces joined together with screws (not small nails), staples, or glue.

THE PROPER *characteristics of a functional nest box.*

- Inside dimensions appropriate for the intended species.

- Dimension of entry hole large enough to admit the targeted species but small enough to prohibit larger nest competitors and predators.

- Outside surfaces painted or stained to be weather-resistant.

- Inside surfaces natural, not painted or stained.

- Roof slanted to shed rain and snow, with a long enough projection in front to overhang the entry hole.

- Small drainage holes in the corners of the floor and larger ventilation holes at the top of the walls, beneath the roof.

- Recessed floor (to help keep water from seeping in the floor seam).

- Be openable, with a front- or side-opening hinged panel for conducting nest inspections (top-opening boxes are harder to check unless you are very tall).

A FEMALE eastern bluebird peeks out of the entrance of a nest box made from PVC pipe and painted to look like a birch tree trunk.

NEST-BOX MOUNTING

Where and how you mount your nest boxes is almost as important as the design of the boxes. In many parts of North America, the spring and summer nesting season for birds is also the time when predators are most active. Nest-box predators are everywhere, so it is important to baffle your nest boxes. Raccoons, chipmunks, mice, squirrels, and other mammals, plus snakes, owls, jays, blackbirds, and crows, will eat eggs or nestlings if they can gain access to your nest boxes. Baffling the boxes will reduce the chances of this happening.

BAFFLES

If you want to be a good landlord to the birds, baffling will be part of your job. Nail a nest box to a tree or fencepost, and you'll feel good about yourself until you see the door ripped off the box and feathers or eggshells (or both!) scattered on the ground below. A predator, likely a raccoon, has climbed up to the nest box, smelled a yummy meal inside, and destroyed the nest box to get at it. Mounting the same box on a length of galvanized pipe, with a stovepipe baffle on the pole beneath it, would have prevented the raccoon from reaching the nest.

BAFFLE TYPES

There are two basic types of predator baffles: pole-mounted baffles and entry-hole baffles. Entry-hole baffles are mounted over the entry hole, extending the distance from the front of the entrance to the inside of the nest box. This deters grackles, owls, jays, and other predators from reaching all the way into the nest box. These baffles do nothing, however, to slow down a determined raccoon or a snake, which glides right past an entry-hole baffle.

The best and easiest way to baffle your boxes is to mount them on galvanized pipe or electrical conduit. This pipe/conduit is held in place vertically by an 8-foot piece of rebar that is pounded into the ground. I use 8-foot sections of ½ inch electrical conduit. I drive 2 feet of the rebar into the ground, slip the conduit down onto the rebar, then mount the nest box at the top of the pipe, at about eye level. I mount the baffle just below the bottom of the nest box. Height is your friend when it comes to mounting the box and baffle because higher boxes are harder for a cat, squirrel, or raccoon to leap onto.

THESE NEST boxes mounted on trees are well built and fully functional, but they lack the protection of predator baffles.

Boxes are typically mounted to poles either on the bottom, using a pipe flange, or on the back, using half-round mounting brackets. "Gilbertson-style" boxes have a ½-inch mounting hole in the roof or bottom to accommodate this pipe-mounting system. No matter how the box mounts to the support pole, it should be mounted firmly enough that the box does not spin or slip up and down.

NO TREES, NO FENCEPOSTS, NO GREASE

Where we live in southeastern Ohio, we share the landscape with many of the most common nest-box predators, but the two we really work to thwart are the raccoon and the black rat snake. On our farm, as in many other places in the eastern, midwestern, and southern U.S., an un-baffled nest box is like a feeder for these animals during the nesting season. Once a raccoon or black rat snake learns that a box on a tree or fencepost regularly contains prey, it will visit repeatedly, cleaning out the contents. Nothing is more upsetting to a nest-box landlord than finding a box that has been raided.

NESTING WOOD ducks on a nest box.

I know bluebird enthusiasts who insist that they have other, easier solutions for preventing their boxes from being raided. One old-timer told me he used axle grease on the bottom of his poles to make them slippery and un-climbable for predators. I'm not a fan of this strategy. For one, the grease melts away over time in the hot sun and pelting rain. Two, axle grease is not something we want coating our local snakes, mammals, pets, or children that might come into contact with the mounting pole. Do yourself a favor and use actual baffles. If you lack the skills to build the simple baffle design in Chapter 7 there are a variety of baffles available commercially. Check your local specialty bird store for details, or search "nest-box predator baffle" online. Some baffles are long, vertical pieces of stovepipe or PVC plastic, whereas others are cone-shaped. I've found that in windy conditions cone-shaped baffles vibrate and clang much more than stovepipe baffles.

An easy-to-make vertical baffle that we've used on our farm, in one form or another, for the past 20 years is on page 189. It's proven to be durable and extremely effective in thwarting climbing predators. Note: It is important to keep the baffle as high up on the mounting pole as possible. Baffles that slip down on the pole allow longer snakes easy access.

Having lectured you on *not* placing nest boxes on trees, I will add that some landlords get away with predator-free "tree" boxes for wrens, woodpeckers, wood ducks, and owls. Where I live, however, this simply won't work.

NEST-BOX PLACEMENT

Placement of any nest boxes you offer depends on the species you hope to attract. Some birds, such as bluebirds, purple martins, and tree and violet-green swallows, prefer a box that's located in the middle of an open field or large lawn. Woodland birds such as chickadees, titmice, and nuthatches prefer nest boxes that are placed in or on the edge of wooded habitat. Carolina, Bewick's, and house wrens prefer edge habitat that is near human habitation. Wood ducks love to nest in boxes placed over water, but they will also use boxes in dryer, wooded habitat, provided the dimensions of the housing are right and there is a body of water nearby. Before placing your nest boxes, decide what birds you want to attract, then research the type of nesting habitat they prefer. The profiles of cavity nesters in Chapter 4 provide some of this information.

SETTING UP A NEST-BOX TRAIL

If you've got appropriate nesting habitat on your property, in your neighborhood, or nearby, it's not too difficult to set up a nest-box trail. The vast majority of the trails set up in North America are devoted to bluebirds, and some of them are pretty extensive to judge by their names: Bluebirds Across Nebraska, Bluebirds Across Montana.

A nest-box trail does not actually have to stretch across an entire state. In fact a trail can include any number of boxes—from two or three to several dozen. The two considerations are placement in appropriate, bird-friendly habitat and the feasibility of regular monitoring. Boxes placed in habitat that is poor for birds from a foraging or safety standpoint are not doing the birds any good. And a nest-box trail with more boxes than a landlord can monitor once weekly is also bad for the birds. Regular monitoring is often the only thing that ensures a high rate of nesting success. Landlords who monitor their boxes can correct problems both inside and outside the nests in a timely fashion. Start with a modest-sized nest-box trail and expand it from there based on your own comfort level.

WOODLAND-LOVING BIRDS *such as chickadees, titmice, woodpeckers, and wrens prefer a nest box placed in or near the woods. Birds such as bluebirds and swallows prefer nests placed in open areas.*

Monitoring Nest Boxes

Conscientious nest-box landlords monitor their nest boxes. While you might worry about disturbing the nesting adults or causing abandonment, the fact is that most cavity nesters will tolerate judicious monitoring very well. And this is a fantastic way to get to know your "tenants" better, and to nip any emerging problems in the bud.

The first step in monitoring is to check your nest boxes regularly. We check ours every few weeks in the winter, just to see if anyone is roosting in them or if they need any repairs.

As the spring nesting season comes on, we watch our nest boxes for activity, and peek inside them about once a week. Our boxes are named for where they are: Side Yard, Middle Meadow, Spring Trail. My wife, Julie, keeps notes for each box in a small field notebook. We're looking for activity such as birds going in and out of the nest box, or a pair of birds perched on the nest box, waving their wings and calling—bluebirds and tree swallows do this at the onset of nest

A LANDLORD *makes notes after a visit to a nest box.*

building. Inside the nest box, we look for bits of nesting material—grass, bark strips, moss, animal fur—as clues that nest building is starting. We note anything we observe on that box's page in the notebook. This helps us keep precise tabs on all the who, what, where, and when of the nesting season.

The eastern bluebirds that nest in several of our 25 or so nest boxes seem to know that we mean no harm when we come to monitor their nests. When we see the nest being lined with soft, fine materials, we know that egg laying will follow soon. Once the first egg is laid (most female songbirds lay one egg per day, usually just after dawn, until the clutch is complete), we begin tallying the progress, checking every few days. During laying, the eggs in the nest will feel cool to the touch. This is because the female will not begin incubating until she has laid her last egg. Once she begins incubating, the eggs will begin developing in response to the warmth of her body.

Checking boxes is easy to do during the midday hours on fair-weather days. During these conditions the adult female will often be away from the nest foraging, so it's possible to check the nest without making her leave. Avoid checking your boxes early and late in the day. Most birds lay eggs in the morning, so it's good to avoid frightening a setting bird.

Here's how a typical nest-box visit might go: Watch the nest from a distance to see any activity. If you've been keeping records, you'll have an idea what stage the nesting process is in. As you approach the nest box, the female may hear you coming and leave. If you suspect she might be inside as you reach the nest, give the outside wall a few scratches with your finger, which may cause her to exit. If you open the box and she is sitting tight, close the box and quietly leave, planning to revisit later. Every nesting bird is slightly different. Some are spookier and shyer than others. Some will scold you loudly as you do your nest check, waiting impatiently for you to leave. Most will watch quietly, and return to the box as soon as you've gone.

WHAT'S INSIDE?

Peeking into an active nest box is a bit like opening a birthday present—you don't always know what you'll see. If things are going well for a nesting pair of birds, you'll see either an adult sitting tight on the nest, or eggs, or hatched young. If you know the date that egg laying ended and incubation began (the first day the eggs were warm to

Here are some terms used to refer to nesting birds:

Brood patch: A patch of bare skin on nesting adult females that facilitates the transfer of her body heat to the eggs or young she is incubating.

Clutch: All the eggs in a single nesting attempt by a pair of birds.

Incubation period: The amount of time that eggs need for development before hatching.

Down: The fine, fluffy feathers that cover nestling birds.

Fledge/fledging day: The day a baby bird leaves the nest.

Fledgling: A young bird that has left the nest.

Hatch/hatching day: The day a bird emerges or hatches from its egg.

Hatchling: A bird that has just emerged from its egg.

Juvenile/juvenal: A bird that is not yet an adult (in plumage, ability to breed, etc.) is called a juvenile bird. Its plumage is referred to as juvenal plumage.

Nestling: A baby bird that is still in the nest.

the touch), then you can estimate the hatching date. A good rule of thumb for nests with hatchlings is to limit your nest visits to the 10 days immediately following hatching. This way you will avoid causing nestlings that are nearly ready to fledge to leave prematurely.

If things are not going well, you'll know that right away too. You may find the nest abandoned because of poor weather and the unavailability of food. Or perhaps the nest was destroyed and the contents eaten by a predator. Perhaps the young fledged earlier than you estimated they would. If this is the case, the nest may look empty and undisturbed. Listen carefully in the habitat around the nest for the sounds of peeping, hungry fledglings. Perhaps the young are still present

A LANDLORD checks a bluebird nest in a nest box.

and seem to be weak or unresponsive. This could be because of cold weather, parasites, or some other environmental factor. This is when you put on your detective cap again and try to solve the riddle of what happened.

There's no substitute for experience if you wish to become a successful nest-box landlord. A great way to learn quickly is to accompany a veteran nest-box landlord or bluebird trail operator on his or

NESTLING TUFTED titmice beg for food.

her monitoring rounds. I've met very few bird landlords who did not take great delight in sharing their knowledge with others. We'll cover nest-box troubleshooting in greater detail in Chapter 5.

DEVELOPMENTAL PHOTOS OF NESTLINGS

These images show the day-by-day development of a Carolina chickadee nest from eggs to almost fledglings. Imagine this: Once all the eggs are laid, they are incubated for 12 to 14 days, they hatch, and 16 to 20 days later, baby chickadees leave the nest box for the first time as fledglings. Think about that: we humans normally take about 18 years to "fledge" from our "nests." And some of us take a lot longer!

CAROLINA CHICKADEE nest on hatching day (Day 1).

DAY 11. Following this day, it's too risky to visit the nest box because it may cause premature fledging (bottom right).

DAY 1

DAY 2

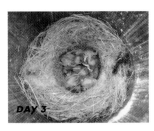
DAY 3

DAY 4

DAY 5

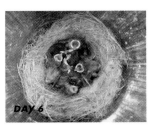
DAY 6

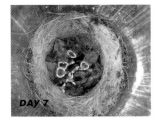
DAY 7

LATER ON DAY 7

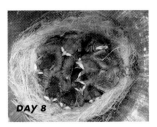
DAY 8

DAY 9

DAY 10

DAY 11

Finding a Baby Bird

It's a race in the natural world to get a nest full of baby birds ready to fledge. Occasionally we find a baby bird on its own in the backyard or along a park path. It looks so helpless and frail. Our heart is screaming at us "Do something! You can't just leave it to be devoured by wild beasts or hit by a car or lawnmower!"

Each spring and summer, millions of baby birds hatch in North America. Most of them will not live long enough to see the next spring. An infinite number of bad things can happen to them, and this is, in part, nature's way of keeping bird populations in balance. Yes, most young birds die, but that does not mean that the one you've just found is doomed if you don't immediately snatch it up and place it in a shoebox.

Many fledglings are perfectly equipped to make it in the world, despite looking lost and helpless to us. In fact, many of

DAY 18. *These Carolina chickadees (from a different nest than those in the previous images) are just about to fledge from the nest.*

them leave their nests before they are fully capable of flying because their chances of survival are much better when they disperse from the nest into nearby habitat.

Perhaps no species is better suited to be the poster child for common, helpless-looking fledglings than the American robin. Fluffy-looking, covered in black dots, hopping around on your lawn, a recently fledged robin looks like the most doomed innocent the world has ever seen. If you resist the urge to scoop it up and instead watch it for an hour or so, you'll see that it is quite mobile, very alert, and probably still being fed by both its parents.

So the best advice, should you encounter a "lost" baby bird, is to leave it alone. Watch it from a distance to satisfy your curiosity. Shoo away a marauding cat or dog if necessary, but unless the bird is injured or in immediate danger, leave it alone.

If the fledgling is injured, or untended by adults, you may want to catch it and put it in a safe place until you can contact a local wild bird or wildlife rehabilitator or rehabilitation center. It is illegal for

MALE WESTERN bluebird.

This information about bluebirds is from Ohio bluebird trail operator—and my wife—Julie Zickefoose, but much of the information she shares is applicable for most orphaned songbirds.

Bluebird Rescue

There will be times as a bluebird landlord when you hit a wall. Either way you go, you may be doing the wrong thing. One of the toughest dilemmas is presented by orphans.

Here's what to do if you find bluebirds that you believe to be orphaned.

First, make sure neither parent is tending the box. This is best done with a continuous watch from a distance. If no adult visits within four hours, you may assume there's trouble. However, if only one parent appears to be tending the young, it may be able to raise them unassisted. If the male disappears, the female will be able to raise the young, for she will brood them at night. The male bluebird, though, lacks this instinct, and though he will feed the young, he won't brood them overnight. He'll be able to keep them alive only if they are more than a week old and the weather is warm. If the chicks are warm to the touch and seem well fed, leave well enough alone. Take them in only if you're sure they're doomed otherwise.

Second, if you must intercede, warm the chicks up with a heating pad set on low or a bottle filled with warm water. They won't be able to gape (open their mouths widely) unless they are warm.

Third, prepare emergency rations. Canned dog food with hard-boiled egg yolk is a good, quick meal. Mold it into small balls, and push them gently into the birds' mouths to stimulate swallowing. A soft whistle may encourage them to gape.

Fourth, locate a licensed wildlife rehabilitator. It's illegal, not to mention very difficult, to raise young birds, which need food every quarter-hour when small. They have a much better chance of surviving with someone who has experience. To find a rehabilitator, call local veterinarians, nature centers, and even pet shops until you find someone who specializes in songbirds. Your state's nongame wildlife division should also keep a list of people with the proper permits for wildlife rehabilitation.

Fifth, try to locate a bluebird trail operator in your area. Someone with a sizable trail usually has several boxes with birds the same age as your orphans. Fostering the nestlings to host nests is the best route of all. Local bird clubs, nature centers, or your state nongame wildlife division might be able to supply you with the name of a trail operator in your state. It's worth the effort, for the orphans' best chance at a normal bluebird life is with real bluebird parents.

AMERICAN ROBIN nestlings about to leave their nest in a hanging basket.

unlicensed individuals to handle or possess wild birds, no matter how good one's intentions. You are permitted to hold an injured bird while transporting it to a licensed rehabber.

Now that we've covered all the high points of providing nest boxes to cavity-nesting birds, let's get to know these birds a bit better.

AN EASTERN screech-owl in a nest box.

Chapter 4: Profiles of Cavity Nesters

A MOUNTAIN chickadee.

IN THIS CHAPTER I'LL SHARE SPECIFIC INFORMATION on the requirements and preferences for the cavity-nesting birds in your backyard. The birds are grouped here for the most part by family since closely related birds mostly share the same housing and habitat requirements. Within each group you'll find the basic type of preferred housing with size specifications, as well as habitat and placement preferences, nest and egg descriptions, incubation and nestling periods, and any interesting behavior or other notable characteristics.

PURPLE MARTIN gourds may be used by roosting birds during the winter months.

Chickadees

CAROLINA CHICKADEE nestlings.

We have seven chickadee species in North America, of which five are regular nest-box users. The other two, gray-headed chickadee (of northern Alaska and the Yukon) and Mexican chickadee (of the mountainous Southwest), have limited breeding ranges, far from human habitation. The five "nest-boxers" are black-capped chickadee, Carolina chickadee, boreal chickadee, chestnut-backed chickadee, and mountain chickadee. Just about anywhere you live in North America, you will find chickadees in appropriate habitat. The boreal chickadee ranges across the forests of the far north, from Canada's maritime provinces to Alaska. The black-capped chickadee overlaps the southern portion of the boreal's range and extends southward from New England in the East, across the middle of the U.S., and through the Rockies to the Pacific Coast. The Carolina chickadee occurs in the southeastern quarter of the U.S., from New Jersey to central Texas and western Oklahoma, south of the largely treeless Great Plains. As its name suggests, the mountain chickadee is found in mountain forests of the West.

The chestnut-backed chickadee is a bird of mountain forests of the Pacific Northwest, from Alaska to California.

All of our chickadees are year-round residents where they occur. They prefer forested or edge habitat, where they forage for insects, spiders, and caterpillars during the warmer months and seeds, nuts, and fruit in winter. Highly energetic and adaptable, chickadees will readily visit feeding stations and use nest boxes for both nesting and roosting. The vast majority of chickadees occupy nesting cavities that a woodpecker has excavated, or that occurs naturally in a tree, or one that they've excavated themselves in soft or rotten wood, using their stout bill as a chisel.

Chickadees nest between the months of March and July and are single-brooded, meaning they produce just one clutch of eggs and raise one brood of young per year. The exception to this rule is when they lose a nest to predation, weather, or some other event. A pair will find a new location and attempt to renest if it is not too late in the breeding season. The nests of chickadees are easy to identify since they almost always incorporate a lot of green moss in the foundation, with a lining of soft fur or hair often gleaned from road-killed mammals.

CHICKADEES AT A GLANCE

Breeding period: March to July

Nest materials: Moss, plant fiber and plant down, wood chips, animal hair or fur, some feathers

Eggs: 6–8, usually white with brownish or red speckles or spots

Incubation: 12–14 days, by female

Hatching to fledging: 16–20 days

CHICKADEE NEST BOX

DIMENSIONS

Interior floor: 4 x 4 or 5 x 5 inches

Interior height: 8–10 inches

Entrance-hole diameter: 1 1/8 – 1 1/2 inches

Height of entrance above floor: 6–7 inches

Placement: At least 5 feet high on a baffled pole

Habitat: Open woods, forest edges, suburban backyards

Interesting Chickadee Tidbits

Opening up a chickadee nest box can be an intriguing experience. The moss foundation and the fur-lined nest cup are beautiful to look at, but it can be difficult to see what's buried deep in the nest. Chickadee females, when they are incubating and must leave the nest to forage, often cover the eggs to keep them both warm and hidden. One other interesting observation I've had with chickadee nests: as active and noisy as chickadees are during most of the year, when they are nesting, they seem to go into stealth mode. As I write this, we've got chickadees nesting in two boxes in our yard, and we rarely, if ever, catch a glimpse of the adults coming and going. This will change, of course, when they have hungry, noisy nestlings to feed.

A TUFTED titmouse gathering soft nesting material.

Birds called "titmice" are our only gray-backed, crested birds—and with their gray face and plain black eyes, they do look rather mouselike. Our five titmouse species are forest birds, like their close relatives the chickadees, and they are also mostly year-round residents wherever they are found. The tufted titmouse is found all across the eastern U.S., from New England to Florida and west to the eastern edge of the mostly treeless Great Plains. The other four titmice species have more limited ranges in the Southwest and West. The black-crested titmouse ranges from southwestern Oklahoma south through central Texas. The bridled titmouse is found in the forested mountains of New Mexico and Arizona. The oak and juniper titmice were formerly one species called plain titmouse, but they have now been split. The juniper titmouse enjoys a large range throughout the interior mountain West. The oak titmouse prefers coastal woodlands from southern Oregon south along the California coast.

Titmice are active, noisy, and gregarious birds. Along with chickadees, they are usually the first birds to visit a new bird feeder or inspect a newly placed nest box, and thus can be attracted as nesting birds. Unlike chickadees, titmice do not do any of their own excavation, even in soft or rotten wood. Instead, they prefer to use old holes excavated by woodpeckers, natural cavities, or a nest box.

The nesting season for our titmice species ranges from March to July. Their nests are similar to chickadee nests, incorporating moss and fur or hair, but titmice also use leaves, grasses, and strips of bark, giving their nests a messier look than those of chickadees. Females do all the nest building.

TITMICE AT A GLANCE

Breeding period: March to July

Nest materials: Moss, plant fiber, bark strips, grasses, leaves, animal hair or fur

Eggs: 6–8, usually white with small brown speckles or dots

Incubation: 12–16 days, by female

Hatching to fledging: 16–21 days

TITMOUSE NEST BOX DIMENSIONS

Interior floor: 4 x 4 or 5 x 5 inches

Interior height: 12 inches

Entrance-hole diameter: 1⅜–1½ inches

Height of entrance above floor: 6+ inches

Placement: At least 5 feet high on a baffled pole

Habitat: Open woods, forest edges, suburban backyards

Interesting Titmice Tidbits

One way to make your yard and nest boxes even more attractive to titmice is to offer a source of fur or hair. Tufted titmice have even been known to snatch hair from sleeping pets and unaware humans. On our farm, we offer mesh bags of alpaca fiber and pet hair during nest building in spring, and the tufted titmice go crazy for it. During courtship and incubation, the male titmouse will feed his mate repeatedly, which helps cement the pair's bond. Later in the nesting cycle, the adult or nestlings may emit a hissing or snapping sound as you peek inside the box. The purpose of this snake imitation is to scare away whatever creature is messing with the nest box. I've even had adult titmice give my hand a nip as I reach inside to feel for eggs.

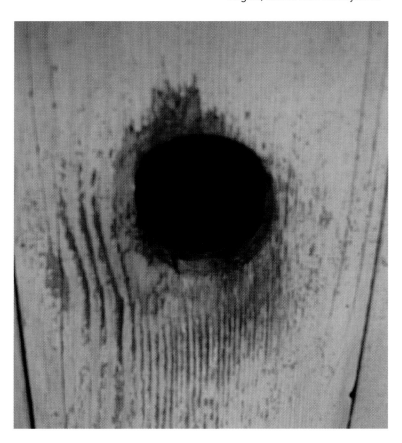

A WOODPECKER has begun enlarging this entry hole on a bluebird box.

Nuthatches

If you read enough about nuthatches, sooner or later you will see them referred to as "nature's wind-up toys." This refers to their jerky, almost mechanical movements as they hitch along tree trunks and over branches seeking their food, which consists of both insects and seeds. The name "nuthatch" comes from this family's habit of wedging a seed into a convenient crevice, then hacking at it with the bill—"hatching" or hacking it open.

Two of our four nuthatches—the pygmy nuthatch of the western mountains and the brown-headed nuthatch of southeastern pine forests—have limited ranges and rarely if ever use nest boxes. The other two more widely distributed nuthatches, the white-breasted and red-breasted, are both regular backyard birds, but only the white-breasted regularly (though infrequently) uses nest boxes. White-breasted nuthatches are year-round residents across

A WHITE-BREASTED nuthatch.

most of North America. Red-breasted nuthatches are year-round residents of the western mountains, but in the East their breeding range is more northerly, and at high elevations in the Appalachian Mountains. In winter the red-breasted migrates southward, and this is when this small bird shows up at feeding stations. All four nuthatch species are known to use nest boxes as nighttime roosts, especially in winter—more on this under Interesting Nuthatch Tidbits.

White-breasted nuthatches prefer to nest in a cavity that's already excavated, rather than do the excavating themselves. The other nuthatches will excavate nesting cavities in rotten wood. The breeding season starts earlier for the white-breasted (March) than for the red-breasted (May), but many of their nesting activities are the same: the female builds a nest in a natural cavity or old woodpecker hole, out of bark shreds, fur or hair, and feathers.

NUTHATCHES AT A GLANCE

Breeding period: March to July

Nest materials: Wood chips, bark strips, rootlets, grasses, animal hair or fur

Eggs: 5–8, usually white with small brown speckles or dots

Incubation: 12 days, by female

Hatching to fledging: 14–21 days

NUTHATCH NEST/ROOST BOX DIMENSIONS

Interior floor: 4 x 4 or 5 x 5 inches

Interior height: 9+ inches

Entrance-hole diameter: 1⅛–1½ inches

Height of entrance above floor: 6+ inches

Placement: At least 5 feet high on a baffled pole.

Habitat: Open mixed woods, forest edges, pine stands, suburban backyards

Interesting Nuthatch Tidbits

On our southeastern Ohio farm, we've had lots of records of white-breasted nuthatches using our blue-bird boxes as winter roost sites, but we've never had a nuthatch nest in one. Our area is rich both with woodpecker species and with old, rotting trees, so the "nutties" have plenty of nest-site options available to them. Elsewhere in North America, both brown-headed and pygmy nuthatches have been recorded roosting in groups in nest boxes, including, in one pygmy nuthatch roost, as many as 100 individuals! Red-breasted nuthatches dab pine sap around the entry hole to their nest to deter predators. White-breasted nuthatches use the same technique, but they use squished blister beetles as the "unwelcome mat."

A CAROLINA wren gathers nesting material.

We have nine wren species in North America, three of which I'll discuss here because they are the only ones that prefer to nest in close proximity to humans: the Carolina, house, and Bewick's wrens. Small, warm brown birds, with short tails often held cocked vertically, wrens are vocal, active bundles of energy and welcome additions to the backyard bird scene.

Wrens prefer shrubby, messy habitat with areas of dense cover where they forage for insects, spiders and spider eggs, caterpillars, and snails. They are loud, persistent singers, and pairs often sing or call back and forth to one another to keep in contact while foraging. All three species build their nests in existing cavities, though some Carolina and Bewick's wrens will build a nest in thick shrubbery rather than inside a cavity. The nests of Bewick's and house wrens are constructed of twigs and lined with grasses and feathers. Carolina wrens make their nests from twigs, grasses, bark strips, moss, and leaves and line them with fur and other soft materials.

The house wren is the smallest of the three and also the most widely distributed, with a range that runs from Canada to Chile. This tiny chocolate brown songster winters in the southernmost U.S. and returns in early spring to its breeding range. It's dark brown above and pale below, with a longish, squared tail that is brown with darker hash marks across it. The bird's voice is a long burbling series of musical notes ringing out over gardens, backyards, and parks. Male house wrens return early and immediately begin building stick nests in every available cavity. When the females return, they select one site for the nest.

A HOUSE wren carries a stick while nest building in a hanging wren house.

The Bewick's wren, a resident of the southwestern and northwestern U.S., is pale, plain gray below and reddish brown above with a bold white eye line. Its long dark tail is edged in white, giving this wren a rather large appearance. This species is declining over much of its range, especially in the eastern portions. The Bewick's song sounds similar to that of a song sparrow.

The Carolina wren is rusty brown above and creamy below, with a pale throat, longish bill, and bold white eye line. It is a noisy, active, year-round resident of the southeastern half of the U.S., where it most commonly nests in and around human habitation. When food is plentiful and nesting successful, this species may raise multiple broods.

WRENS AT A GLANCE

Breeding period: March to August

Nest materials: Base of sticks (Bewick's and house wrens), lined with fine grasses, plant fiber, fur, feathers, and bark strips; moss, grasses, leaves, lined with animal hair or fur (Carolina wren)

Eggs: 6–8, usually white with dark speckles

Incubation: 12–15 days, by female

Hatching to fledging: 16–21 days

WREN NEST BOX

DIMENSIONS

Interior floor: 4 x 4 or 5 x 5 inches

Interior height: 9+ inches

ENTRANCE-HOLE DIAMETER

House wren: 1–1½ inches

Bewick's wren: 1¼–1½ inches

Carolina wren: 1½ inches

Height of entrance above floor: 4 to 6+ inches

Placement: 6 or more feet high on a building or baffled pole (preferred)

Habitat: Open areas, forest edges, suburban backyards, gardens, brush piles; house wrens prefer to be away from deep woods

Interesting Wren Tidbits

Belying their small size, house wrens often destroy the eggs of other cavity-nesting birds by piercing them and removing them from the cavity. This is thought to be super-competitive behavior designed to keep viable nest sites from being used by other birds. Male house wrens typically build nests in several cavities in a yard or patch of habitat. The female of a mated pair chooses one of these nests to use. However, the "dummy" nests often render the cavity or nest box unusable because they are filled up with twigs. Landlords that remove house wren nests as they are being built risk experiencing the wrens' "revenge" in the form of egg destruction in neighboring nests. Once a house wren nest is built and has eggs in it, it is safe for a landlord to remove the adjacent dummy nests.

Interesting Swallow Tidbits

Tree and violet-green swallows prefer to line their nests with soft white feathers, and they may fly miles away to find a good source, such as a poultry farm. During nest building you can offer white craft feathers to your backyard swallows. We've even had one or two bold tree swallows swoop in to take the feathers from our hands.

Violet-green swallows have been observed helping western bluebirds raise their young to fledging, with the swallows taking over the nest cavity upon the bluebirds' departure.

The violet-green swallow, which breeds in the western third of North America, and the tree swallow, which breeds across much of North America, are the only two swallow species that regularly use nest boxes. Both breed during the warmer months of the year, coinciding with the availability of flying insects, their primary food. Another member of the swallow family, the purple martin, is heavily dependent on human-supplied housing for nesting. However, the martin's nesting habits and requirements are different enough to be handled separately from these other two swallow species.

Violet-green swallows can be found almost anywhere in the West in summer, from the Rocky Mountains to the Pacific Ocean and from central Alaska south to Mexico. Adults are bright glossy green above with a purple rump and upper tail. Bright white below, the violet-green swallow has a clean white face and two crescents of white on either side of the rump. This species breeds in open woodlands with standing dead wood and abundant woodpecker cavities, but it will readily accept nest boxes in suburban settings.

Adult male tree swallows are teal blue-green above and pure

A MALE tree swallow.

white below with a dark face. Females are similar but are duller blue or brown above. Tree swallows prefer open grassy habitat near water, and where there are abundant nest sites, they may form loose colonies. Both tree and violet-green swallows have a notched tail and are very vocal during the nesting season.

Both of these species return in early spring and nest from April through early July. The relatively early nesting cycle can affect spring broods adversely. If poor weather makes foraging for flying insects impossible, adults will save themselves by leaving to find food elsewhere, which means abandoning nests. Often, when the weather and foraging improve, they return to finish incubating the eggs. If poor weather persists and the nesting attempt fails, both species, and especially tree swallows, will attempt a second nesting. By late summer these swallows have begun migrating to their wintering grounds in more tropical climes.

TREE SWALLOW nests usually have white or pale feathers in them.

SWALLOWS AT A GLANCE

Breeding period: April to July

Nest materials: Grasses and straw, lined with soft feathers

Eggs: 4–6, pure white

Incubation: 13–15 days, by female

Hatching to fledging: 21 days

SWALLOW NEST BOX DIMENSIONS

Interior floor: 4 x 4 or 5 x 5 inches

Interior height: 9–12 inches

Entrance-hole diameter: 1¼–1½ inches

Height of entrance above floor: 6+ inches

Placement: 5–6 feet high on a baffled pole

Habitat: Open areas near water; forest edges; large, open suburban backyards; parks; golf courses

Purple Martin

A MALE purple martin.

Interesting Martin Tidbits

It was once argued (by an enterprising martin house manufacturer) that purple martins were "America's most-wanted bird!" because he claimed that a single purple martin ate 3,000 mosquitoes per day. The truth is that martins don't eat insects as small as mosquitoes when there is larger, more filling fare around, such as dragonflies, flying ants, beetles, June bugs, and crane flies. Besides, most mosquitoes come out at dusk, after all the martins have gone to roost.

If you read Chapter 3 of this book, you're already familiar with the close historical relationship between humans and purple martins in the eastern U.S. This largest North American member of the swallow family nests almost exclusively in human-supplied housing across most of eastern North American and western Canada. Some populations in the desert Southwest and Pacific Northwest still nest in natural cavities or old woodpecker holes. Purple martins capture their food (flying insects) in flight, so they prefer open areas where such foraging is possible.

Adult male purple martins are dark purple-blue overall (in fact, this is our only dark-bellied swallow) with a deeply notched tail and triangular wing shape in flight. Females and young birds are grayish overall with a gray collar and a messy gray chest. Adult females show a patch of dark blue on the crown and back. Purple martins are very social, preferring to nest in a colony with multiple other pairs—some martin colonies have hundreds of birds. The birds prefer open habitat near both human habitation and water, and they are very particular in their nest site and housing preferences.

Martins will nest in hollowed-out natural gourds, in molded plastic gourds, in wooden multi-compartment houses, and in metal condo-type houses. The housing needs to be painted white or a light color. Martins prefer this, though the reasons for this preference are debated. Perhaps the white color keeps the inside of the nest box cooler in direct summer sun, and it certainly makes the dark entrance hole stand out. It should be placed within 100 feet of human habitation and should be the highest object in the immediate area. It should be baffled against predators from below and should be able to be raised and lowered. Finally, it should have nest compartments that can be opened for monitoring and cleaning. This last requirement is important because many martin colonies are beset by non-native house sparrows

PURPLE MARTIN houses can attract more martins with the addition of nearby perches.

competing for nest cavities. Most martin landlords remove house sparrow nests as soon as they are built, harassing or dispatching the offending interlopers.

PURPLE MARTINS AT A GLANCE

Breeding period: April to August

Nest materials: Grasses, small twigs, pine needles, leaves, feathers, mud

Eggs: 5–6, pure white

Incubation: 15–16 days, by female

Hatching to fledging: 26–31 days

MARTIN NEST BOX DIMENSIONS

Interior floor: 6 x 6 inches or larger

Interior height: 6 inches

Entrance-hole diameter: 2⅛ inches (many martin landlords favor specialized starling-resistant holes; see the Resources section for informative martin websites)

Height of entrance above floor: 1 inch

Placement: 10–20 feet high on a baffled pole

Habitat: Open areas near human habitation and water

Bluebirds

A PAIR of western bluebirds at their nest box.

Our three bluebird species are found primarily where their names suggest they might be. Eastern bluebirds range over the entire eastern U.S. and southern Canada. Western bluebirds are found throughout much of the West, except at the highest elevations, a habitat that is preferred by the mountain bluebird, which nests from central Alaska east to the Dakotas and south to the southwestern mountains.

Males of both eastern and western bluebirds are a combination of bright sky blue head, back, wings, and tail; rusty breast; and white belly. Male westerns, however, usually show some rust on the shoulders and across the upper back. Male mountain bluebirds are pale blue overall with a white belly. Females of all three species have duller plumages that faintly echo the males' look.

Bluebirds readily accept human-supplied housing throughout their range, and in fact they owe much of their population stability and expansion to the thousands of bluebird trail operators across the continent who have erected and maintained millions of nest boxes specifically for bluebirds. (See Chapter 3 for the background on this conservation success story.) Members of the thrush family, bluebirds possess musical songs, which delight those of us who host these beauties. Despite their vast ranges and population

FAMILY OF eastern bluebird enjoying mealworms.

A TYPICAL bluebird nest box in open habitat with a predator baffle.

Young bluebirds from a successful spring nesting may stick around to help their parents with the care and feeding of later broods. Mountain bluebirds are the most migratory of the three species, moving to lower elevation wintering grounds where they may form foraging flocks of up to 100 birds. Many eastern and western bluebirds migrate only when harsh weather reduces the availability of natural food resources. In areas of the far north and the West where snakes and climbing predatory mammals are not common, many landlords do not baffle nest boxes. In my opinion, it's always best to use a predator baffle— better safe than sorry.

success, bluebirds do not nest everywhere. They need open, grassy space for foraging and prefer to nest nearby in habitat with, at most, scattered trees. For this reason, would-be bluebird landlords with wooded backyards are often frustrated in their attempts to host bluebirds. Where bluebirds do nest in suburban neighborhood settings, their nesting success may be foiled by the use of lawn chemicals, which are highly toxic to nestlings and adults.

Where appropriate habitat does exist, chances are excellent for attracting nesting bluebirds if the proper housing is available. Bluebirds will readily nest in old woodpecker holes or natural cavities in trees, but in many areas their best reproductive success comes from nesting in human-supplied housing. There is no single, ideal bluebird box, despite claims to the contrary. Bluebird preferences vary with individual nesting pairs, as well as with environmental factors such as the presence of nest-site competitors, such as European starlings and house sparrows, and nest-box predators.

The basic bluebird nest box has become the default standard for cavity-nesting birds, since the dimensions of the entry hole (1 ½ inches in diameter) and interior, as well as the placement in

MALE MOUNTAIN bluebird on a lilac branch.

the habitat, suit a number of species that are bluebird-sized and smaller. Entry holes of 1½ inches for eastern bluebirds and 1⁹/₁₆ inches for mountain and western bluebirds will exclude European starlings from entering.

Bluebirds nest from March through July or August. Females build the nest out of dried grasses, pine needles, rootlets, and bark strips and line it with softer materials such as hair or feathers. All three species have been recorded producing multiple broods in a single nesting season.

BLUEBIRDS AT A GLANCE

Breeding period: March to August

Nest materials: Grasses, small twigs, pine needles, rootlets, bark strips, lined with soft grasses, feathers, and hair

Eggs: 3–8, blue, pale blue, or whitish

Incubation: 14 days, by female

Hatching to fledging: Up to 21 days

BLUEBIRD NEST BOX

(See the Resources section for informative bluebird websites and organizations.)

DIMENSIONS

Interior floor:

Eastern: 4 x 4 inches

Western: 5 x 5 inches

Mountain: 5½ x 5½ inches

Interior height: 12 inches

Entrance-hole diameter:

Eastern: 1½ inches

Western: 1½ inches; where range overlaps mountain bluebird, use 1⁹/₁₆ inches

Mountain: 1⁹/₁₆ inches

Height of entrance above floor: 6+ inches

Placement: 4–6 feet high on baffled metal pole; predators can easily access boxes placed on trees and fenceposts

Habitat: Open grassy habitat, fields, parks, roadsides with scattered snags for perches

American Robin

Although it is a member of the thrush family, as are our three bluebird species, the American robin does not nest inside a cavity, but it often nests near humans in landscape trees and shrubs, under eaves, and on windowsills. This makes sense, since much of the food that robins eat comes in the form of earthworms from lawns and grassy areas, as well as from fruits of ornamental plantings in fall and winter.

Famous bird authority Roger Tory Peterson, in his first field guide, referred to the American robin as "the one bird that everybody knows." The

AN AMERICAN robin.

robin's brick red breast and dark back are a familiar sight on lawns in spring and summer all across North America. The male has a darker back and is more boldly colored than the female.

Robins seem at home in a variety of habitats, as long as there is grassy foraging habitat and cover for nesting nearby. The nest, built by the pair, is a sturdy cup of twigs, grasses, and mud, lined with finer, softer grass.

ROBINS AT A GLANCE

Breeding period: March to August

Nest materials: Grasses, bark strips, sticks, mud

Eggs: 3–7, blue or pale blue

Incubation: 14 days, by female

Hatching to fledging: Up to 16 days

ROBIN NEST SHELF

Dimensions: A flat board measuring 6 x 6 inches with 2-inch-high side walls

Placement: Under eaves or against a wall in some protected place

Habitat: Open grassy habitat, parks, suburban backyards

Interesting Robin Tidbits

Many bird lovers (and even more nonbirders) hail the "first robin of spring" each year. In reality, robins do not always make a long migration, especially in areas with mild winters. Foraging flocks of robins spend winters in wooded habitat and emerge to forage on lawns when the weather breaks and the ground is soft enough for earthworms to be active.

Flycatchers

GREAT CRESTED *flycatcher nests often have a shed snakeskin hanging out of the entrance, to deter predators.*

Two of our North America flycatchers regularly use nest boxes: the great crested flycatcher, common in summer in eastern North America, and the ash-throated flycatcher, a western counterpart that nests from Oregon south to California and east to central Texas. Three other flycatcher family members are known to build nests in or on buildings, in culverts, and under bridges: Say's phoebe, black phoebe, and eastern phoebe. Although none of these species use nest boxes, they can be encouraged to nest near or on human habitation within their breeding range through the placement of robin nesting platforms as described above.

Both of our cavity-nesting flycatchers are secondary cavity nesters, meaning they do not excavate their own nest holes. Being fairly large birds, they need large

CAVITY-NESTING FLYCATCHERS *must rely on existing holes for nesting.*

cavities for nesting. Their most common nesting sites are in natural cavities in trees or, occasionally, in old woodpecker holes. Both species are similar in appearance: gray-olive head, gray breast, pale yellow belly, and long rusty brown tail. They often show a bit of rufous in the wings and tail. Their preferred habitat is deciduous woods and adjacent edge habitat, parks, and orchards. The birds' drab colors help them blend into the surrounding habitat, but their frequent loud vocalizations assure that they are often heard before they are seen.

A mated pair will select a nest cavity in appropriate habitat and fill it nearly to the opening with grasses, leaves, hair, fur, and often a snakeskin.

FLYCATCHERS AT A GLANCE

Breeding period: March to July

Nest materials: Grasses, pine needles, bark strips, fur, hair, and often snakeskins

Eggs: 4–6, off-white, blotched with brown or purple

Incubation: 15 days, by female

Hatching to fledging: Up to 21 days

FLYCATCHER NEST BOX DIMENSIONS

Interior floor: 5 x 5 or 6 x 6 inches

Interior height: 9–12 inches

Entrance-hole diameter: 1½ inches (everywhere) to 2½ inches (where European starlings are not a problem)

Height of entrance above floor: 6+ inches

Placement: 6–18 feet high on baffled metal pole or high up on a large deciduous tree; note that predators can easily access boxes placed on trees and fenceposts

Habitat: Woodlands and woodland edge, groves, parks, cemeteries, open habitat with scattered clumps of trees

Interesting Flycatcher Tidbits

Why do these flycatchers (and a few other species, such as some titmice) use snakeskins in their nests? There are two primary hypotheses: One is that the snakeskins deter nest predators, such as squirrels, flying squirrels, and other birds, that may be afraid of snakes. The second hypothesis is that the crinkly, flexible, durable snakeskins simply make excellent nesting material, since some flycatcher nests have been found to have cellophane and even wax paper in them. One study did show that southern flying squirrels were less likely to raid a flycatcher nest that had obvious snakeskin in it.

Woodpeckers

Interesting Woodpecker Tidbits

Because of the long post-fledging period for many woodpeckers, youngsters are often seen following their parents around, begging for food. This is a common sight at our southeastern Ohio bird feeders in late summer, where we feed downy, hairy, and red-bellied woodpeckers.

Woodpecker heads and brains are designed to withstand almost constant pounding as the birds excavate for food and cavities, and as males drum during courtship. The brain fits tightly within the skull, and the skull structure is such that it prevents the brain from moving in response to the force of a woodpecker's bill striking a hard surface.

A GOLDEN-FRONTED woodpecker.

Our woodpeckers are natural-born excavators. You'd think that, gifted by nature with sharp, powerful, chisel-like bills and the power and endurance to drill large nesting holes in the hard wood of large trees, woodpeckers might never have a reason to use a nest box. But some of our woodpeckers do use nest boxes. They include northern flicker, red-headed woodpecker, golden-fronted woodpecker, red-bellied woodpecker, hairy woodpecker, and downy woodpecker.

The largest of these species is the northern flicker, a bird that is about a foot in length from bill tip to tail tip. Flickers are warm brown overall with thin horizontal stripes across the back, black dots on the pale breast, and a necklace of black. Male flickers sport a mustache, black in eastern (yellow-shafted) birds and red in western (red-shafted) birds. In flight, flickers show either yellow underwings and undertail (eastern yellow-shafted form) or red underwings and undertail (western red-shafted form). They are very noisy birds year-round and are often seen on the ground foraging for their favorite food: ants. They are common all across North America in open woods, parks, and suburban neighborhoods.

Adult red-headed woodpeckers have an all-red head and hood and are bright white below, with large patches of black and white on the back and wings. In flight, this black-white-black pattern is hard to miss, even at great distances. Red-headed woodpeckers love open woods, especially those with oaks and other nut-bearing trees. These birds are locally common in summer across much of the eastern U.S. They are excellent at flycatching and will often sit quietly for long periods waiting for an insect to fly within reach.

Red-bellied and golden-fronted woodpeckers are close relatives, though the former is common in woodlands, parks, and towns throughout the East and Southeast whereas the latter ranges throughout central Texas in mesquite groves and woodlands. Both have a zebra-striped back, plain gray front, and show a white rump in flight. Males have a red crown. Male golden-fronteds also have a patch of bright yellow at the upper base of the bill and on the nape.

Downy and hairy woodpeckers also resemble each other in appearance: the body, tail, wings, and head show bold patterns of black and white, with males sporting a small red patch at the back of the head. Hairy woodpeckers average larger than downies, with a longer body, larger head, and longer

A FEMALE downy woodpecker.

bill. Both are common year-round residents across the continent in forests, open woodlands, parks, and suburban yards. They are more likely to use nest boxes for winter roosting sites than for spring and summer nesting sites.

In very general terms, the breeding season for these woodpeckers runs from April through July or August. After courtship, which includes lots of loud calling, chasing, and drumming, a mated pair will excavate a nest cavity. Once it's finished, the female will lay four or five pure white eggs (flicker clutches are often larger), and both sexes will share the two-week incubation duties. Nestlings will remain in the cavity for as much as a month before fledging. Post-fledging care of young birds by the parents may continue for anywhere from three weeks to two months.

WOODPECKERS AT A GLANCE

Breeding period: April to August

Nest materials: None

Eggs: 4–5, unmarked white

Incubation: 11–14 days, by male and female

Hatching to fledging: Up to 30 days

LARGE WOODPECKER NEST BOX (FOR NORTHERN FLICKER)

DIMENSIONS:

Interior floor: 6 x 6 inches or larger

Interior height: 14–20 inches

Entrance-hole diameter: 2+ inches

Height of entrance above floor: 10 inches or more

Placement: 10–20 feet high on baffled metal pole or tree; predators can easily access boxes placed on trees

Habitat: Forested habitat, woodland edge

MEDIUM WOODPECKER NEST BOX (FOR OTHER SPECIES)

DIMENSIONS

Interior floor: 5 x 5 inches or larger

Interior height: 14–16 inches

Entrance-hole diameter: 1¾–2¾ inches (use smaller size where starlings are a problem)

Height of entrance above floor: 10 inches

Placement: 6–18 feet high on baffled metal pole or tree; predators can easily access boxes placed on trees

Habitat: Forested habitat, woodland edge

Owls

Often the first sign that you have owls in or near your backyard is when you hear them calling after dark. Many people would be surprised to know just how common many of our North American owls are—you probably have at least one species, and perhaps two or three, living in your immediate surroundings. But because owls are largely nocturnal, we diurnal-living humans rarely see them. Most of our North American owl species nest in cavities, but only five of these commonly use human-supplied nest boxes: the northern saw-whet owl, eastern and western screech-owls, barred owl, and barn owl. Other owls that I have seen using human-supplied housing include boreal owl, elf owl, and burrowing owl (which regularly uses artificial underground burrows). However, these species are too rare, limited in range, or specialized in their housing requirements to be included here.

AN EASTERN screech-owl roosts in a hollow in a locust tree.

The more common nest-box-using owls cover a range of sizes, from the tiny northern saw-whet (8 inches tall) to the barred owl (21 inches tall), as well as a range of habitats. Eastern and western screech-owls are habitat generalists that are just as at home in a wooded suburban backyard as they are in a remote wooded canyon. Barn owls prefer to live near open grassland where they can fly low over fields and meadows listening and watching for small mammals. Barred owls are found in wet deciduous woods, swamps, and river bottoms. Northern saw-whet owls prefer dense mixed forest, wooded swamps, and bogs. Before placing housing for these species, check a field guide to see which species occur near you, then place the housing in the appropriate habitat.

The nesting season for these owl species runs from March through July. Clutch sizes range from two or three (barred owl) to as many as six (barn and northern saw-whet). Owl eggs are white and require about a month of incubation, which is sometimes a shared duty between mates. After leaving the nest, young owls receive parental support for many weeks, and this is when both young and adults are most visible and active.

Eastern and western screech-owls are small owls with obvious tufts on their head and bright yellow eyes with black pupils. They nest and roost in cavities, often sticking their head out to catch the warmth of the sun or to peek out at approaching danger. Both species come in a mottled gray and black plumage—which perfectly mimics tree bark and is excellent camouflage. Easterns also occur in a red morph.

The northern saw-whet owl is a small chocolate brown and caramel-colored owl, lacking ear tufts. It has a white breast heavily streaked with rust, and its large yellow eyes stand out in its facial disc. Its name comes from its call, which sounds like the high-pitched whistle a saw makes when it is being sharpened with a metal file. This shy, quiet bird nests at high elevations in the forested mountains of the East and West. Little is known about its migration patterns.

The barred owl's call of *Who cooks for YOU! Who cooks for YOU-all* is a common sound throughout woodlands in eastern North America as well as in the far north and the Northwest. Large and gray-brown overall, the barred owl has mottled plumage that helps it blend into the dappled light of its habitat. It has large dark eyes surrounded by a circular facial disc. It is a year-round resident wherever it occurs.

A BARN owl adult and nestlings.

Barn owls were once common nesting birds across the southern half of the U.S., nesting, as the name suggests, in barns and silos. As farmland habitat was converted to suburban housing, and the standard old, open wooden barns were replaced by windowless metal structures, barn owls suffered a severe decline. Called the "monkey-faced owl" for its heart-shaped, white facial disc surrounding two dark eyes, the barn owl is yellowish tan above and white, with fine dark spots, below. It is often heard giving its loud grating rasp of a call that one friend of mine insists should be the sound for midnight on the Bird Clock from Hell. Barn owls are year-round residents across much of their range, but northern nesting birds migrate south in late fall.

THIS PELLET from an eastern screech-owl contains the bill and feathers of a northern cardinal.

OWLS AT A GLANCE

Breeding period: March to July

Nest materials: None

Eggs: 2–6, round, white

Incubation: 30+/- days, by male and female

Hatching to fledging: 60+ /- days

LARGE OWL NEST BOX (FOR BARRED AND BARN OWLS)
DIMENSIONS

Interior floor:

Barn: 16 x 22 inches

Barred: 14 x 14 inches

Interior height: 16 inches (barn) to 22+ inches (barred)

Entrance-hole diameter: 6+ inches (taller than wide, if hole is larger)

Height of entrance above floor: 14+ inches (barred), 4 inches (barn)

Placement: 10–20 feet high on a tree (barred owl) or in a barn or silo (barn owl)

Habitat: Woodlands near water, swamps (barred); open farmland (barn)

SMALL OWL NEST BOX (FOR SCREECH-OWLS AND NORTHERN SAW-WHET OWL)
DIMENSIONS

Interior floor: 6 x 6 inches or larger

Interior height: 14–18 inches

Entrance-hole diameter: 2¾–4 inches

Height of entrance above floor: 10+ inches

Placement: 6–20 feet high on baffled metal pole or tree

Habitat: Suburban or rural woodland edge, orchards (screech-owls); thick forest near water, swamps (northern saw-whet owl)

FEMALE AMERICAN
Kestrel

A NESTING *pair of American kestrels.*

Our smallest falcon, the American kestrel, is the only cavity-nesting hawk that regularly uses nest boxes. Some of the large green road signs along interstate highways here in the Midwest have kestrel nest boxes affixed to the back side, which is perfect, since the kestrel is one of our continent's most common roadside hawks. Kestrels are often seen hovering in place, looking on the ground below for the movement of potential prey, such as mice and other small rodents, songbirds, snakes and lizards, grasshoppers, and other large insects. When perched, kestrels regularly pump their tail—a good way to identify this small falcon. Male kestrels are a handsome mix of rusty orange on the crown, chest, back, and tail, with blue-gray wings and a white face bisected by a black double mustache. Young birds and females are lighter rust and streaked with brown overall.

Kestrels are present year-round across most of the U.S., and in summers they breed as far north as northern Canada and central Alaska. The breeding season lasts from April through June. Pairs select a nesting cavity in an old woodpecker hole, a hole in a building, or a nest box.

AMERICAN KESTRELS AT A GLANCE

Breeding period: April to June

Nest materials: None

Eggs: 4–5, white or pinkish white with brown spots

Incubation: 30 days, by female

Hatching to fledging: 30 days

MALE AMERICAN Kestrel at nest hollow.

AMERICAN KESTREL NEST BOX DIMENSIONS:

Interior floor: 8 x 8 inches

Interior height: 14–18 inches

Entrance-hole diameter: 3 inches

Height of entrance above floor: 10+ inches

Placement: 12–30 feet high on baffled metal pole, utility pole, or building; beware of placing kestrel nest boxes too close to other active nest boxes since kestrels do prey on songbirds

Habitat: Open grassy habitat, hayfields, parks, roadsides, woodland edges

Interesting American Kestrel Tidbits

Older field guides may refer to the American kestrel as the sparrow hawk. While this species does prey on songbirds and even sparrows, its dietary mainstays are small mammals such as mice and voles, small snakes, and large insects such as cicadas and grasshoppers. Adult kestrels teach their young to hunt by example, sometimes capturing prey and dropping it from a perch onto the ground for the young to practice with.

Prothonotary Warbler

A FEMALE prothonotary warbler in the nest cavity.

Two North American warbler species are known cavity nesters, the prothonotary warbler and Lucy's warbler. The prothonotary warbler is a summer nester in wooded swamps in the Midwest, South, and Southeast and in southernmost Ontario, where it readily takes to nest boxes placed in proper habitat. Lucy's warbler is not known to use nest boxes at all.

It's hard to miss a male prothonotary warbler. Its golden yellow plumage and dark wings, back, and tail are visually striking. And its loud, ringing song, *sweet-sweet-sweet-sweet-sweet*, is easily heard in the still air of its favored habitat in heavily wooded swamps. Competition for nesting cavities can be severe in this habitat, where tree swallows, bluebirds, titmice, wrens, chickadees, European starlings, kestrels, eastern screech-owls, and even house sparrows may all be fighting over a limited number of natural cavities or old woodpecker holes. This is why nest boxes placed specifically for this species in swampy backwaters and wooded river ways have produced excellent nesting success.

Prothonotary warblers return from Central and South America in early spring and nest from April through June. Once a pair finds a nesting cavity, which is almost always in a tree that is surrounded by water or in a flooded area, the female improves the cavity with moss, leaves, and bark strips and lines it with fine grasses. In the southern parts of the prothonotary's range, the pair may attempt a second brood.

PROTHONOTARY WARBLERS AT A GLANCE

Breeding period: April to June

Nest materials: Moss, dry leaves, twigs, bark strips, fine grasses

Eggs: 3–8, white splotched with brown

Incubation: 12–14 days, by female

Hatching to fledging: 14 days

PROTHONOTARY WARBLER NEST BOX

DIMENSIONS

Interior floor: 4 x 4 inches

Interior height: 9–12 inches

Entrance-hole diameter: 1¼ inches

Height of entrance above floor: 5+ inches

Placement: 4–6 feet high on baffled metal pole placed in standing water or on tree trunk in swampy or flooded area

Habitat: Wooded swamps, river bottoms, ponds, flooded bottomland

Interesting Prothonotary Warbler Tidbits

Fledgling prothonotary warblers may not be able to fly well enough to make it to a safe perch from the nest cavity. But they have the instinctive ability to "swim" using their legs and wings, scooting across the surface of the water to the safety of a nearby log or bit of dry land. The name of this species is a reference, reportedly first used by Creoles in Louisiana in the eighteenth century, to the golden robes worn by a high official in the Catholic church—the protho-notary or protho-notarius.

A MALE wood duck.

With all of these cavity-nesting duck species, the ducklings leave the nest within a day of hatching, but before they are developed enough to fly—in fact they are still covered only in down! They accomplish this by leaping from the nest and floating to the ground—which can be a drop of more than 50 feet. They are able to do this because they are so light that they drift down slowly to a soft, tumbled landing, after which they follow their mom to the nearest body of water.

Ducks use nest boxes? Ducks nest in cavities? It may seem strange, but several of our common North American waterfowl species use cavities for nesting. Because waterfowl management for hunting has been so well studied, we know quite a bit about the natural history and nesting preferences of these cavity-nesting ducks, including how to properly provide nest boxes for them. If you think of a duck that nests in a cavity, it might be the wood duck. In fact, if you've ever seen a huge nest box with a grapefruit-sized entry hole, mounted on a pole in a swamp, it was almost certainly placed there for wood ducks.

Our cavity-nesting ducks are the wood duck, Barrow's and common goldeneyes, bufflehead, common and hooded mergansers, and black-bellied whistling-duck. Of these, the wood duck enjoys the widest distribution, nesting all across the continent from southern Canada to Mexico, with the exception of the southwestern quadrant of the U.S. The goldeneyes and bufflehead winter in the U.S. but nest primarily in the boreal regions of the far north. Common and hooded mergansers breed in the northeastern and northwestern quadrants of the continent, the hooded merganser being more widely distributed in the East and the common merganser in the West. The black-bellied whistling-duck breeds in ponds and swamps in southeastern Arizona, central and coastal Texas, and sparingly elsewhere along the Gulf of Mexico and in central Florida.

All of these ducks need large cavities for nesting—either natural holes in trees, cavities excavated by pileated woodpeckers, or nest boxes. Years of study of ducks nesting in nest boxes have produced some recommendations for increased success. Boxes placed over water should be at least 4 feet above the water's surface and, if pole-mounted, should have a predator baffle beneath the box.

Boxes placed in trees should be near the water and at least 10 feet above the ground to make them harder for predators to locate. Make sure nesting adults will have a clear flight path to and from the box. Inside the box, several inches of dry wood chips placed on the floor will provide a stable cushion as well as insulation for eggs and young. Chiseled-out grooves on the inside front of the nest box, below the entrance hole, will help ducklings depart safely at fledging time. It also helps to mount the box so that it is tilted forward.

By far the most colorful of our cavity-nesting ducks is the male wood duck, which sports a stunning harlequin pattern of green, red, orange, purple, tan, and black. In all of these cavity-nesting ducks, females incubate the eggs for up to six weeks, and the time from hatching to fledging is a single day.

A NESTLING wood duck, just one day old, leaps to the ground from the nest cavity.

DUCKS AT A GLANCE

Breeding period: April to July

Nest materials: Down and feathers that the female plucks from her breast

Eggs: 8–14; color varies by species from white to buff to pale green

Incubation: 27–35 days, by female

Hatching to fledging: 1 day

WOOD DUCK NEST BOX
(ALSO FOR LARGER DUCKS)

DIMENSIONS:

Interior floor: 10 x 10 to 12 x 12 inches

Interior height: 24 inches

Entrance-hole diameter:

Wood duck, hooded merganser: 3 inches high x 4 inches wide

Goldeneyes, black-bellied whistling-duck: 3½ inches high x 4½ inches wide

Common merganser: 4 inches high x 5 inches wide

Height of entrance above floor: 16+ inches

Placement: 4+ feet high on baffled metal pole placed over water; boxes placed on trees should be near water with a clear flight path and at least 10–20 feet high

Habitat: Wooded habitat near water: swamps, lakes, sloughs, ponds

European Starling and House Sparrow

A EUROPEAN starling.

Both of these cavity-nesting species are non-native birds that were brought to North America from Europe by misguided humans. Both the starling and house sparrow did so well here that they soon began to outcompete our native cavity nesters for nest sites. Thriving in a variety of habitats, from the most urban to the most rural, these birds are considered enemies by many nest-box landlords because of their success in driving off and even killing (in the case of house sparrows) native cavity nesters. Most dedicated nest-box landlords do not tolerate the presence of either species nesting in boxes intended for native species. Removing the nest, plugging the entry hole, and even killing the nesting adult house sparrows or starlings are all strategies employed by landlords—and all are permitted by law since these are non-native species.

Male house sparrows (sometimes referred to in older references as English sparrows) are medium-sized, chunky-looking sparrows with a gray head, chestnut nape, and black bib. Females are plain brown with a faint eye line. Throughout the nesting season (March through August), male house sparrows utter a *chi-deep* call repeatedly, from on or near the nest site. A male and his mate build a messy nest of grass, weed stems, feathers, hair, and even bits of trash. There is often so much material that the nest curves up and

A MALE *house sparrow.*

over, forming a roof inside the nest cavity. The female lays four to six white eggs, spotted with brown flecks, and incubates them for 12 days. Nestlings develop over the next two or more weeks before fledging.

European starlings appear glossy purplish green speckled with white, with a yellow bill during the breeding season. In fall they become paler, browner, and more speckled. They are amazing singers and mimics, making a huge variety of sounds, including whistles, buzzes, rattles, and chuckles. Any cavity will do for nesting starlings—holes in trees, buildings, and any nest box with an entry hole large enough for them to fit through. The nest is started by the male and finished by the female and is composed of grasses, weed stems, twigs, rootlets, bits of string, paper, and moss, and it's lined with fine grasses. The female lays four to six pale blue eggs, and both adults share the 12-day incubation duty. Fledging occurs about 24 days later.

Both of these aggressive, highly adaptable birds will nest wherever they can. If you wish to thwart them, the information in the next chapter will help.

Chapter 5: Troubleshooting and FAQs

CHECKING NESTS *in nest boxes is perfectly all right up until the nestlings near fledging age. (See the "Hatching to fledging" days given throughout Chapter 4.)*

IN THE PREVIOUS FOUR CHAPTERS I've covered a lot of ground about how to make things right for nesting birds in your backyard. The trouble is, there's trouble sometimes. In this chapter I'll try to help you steer clear of trouble, or solve any problems you encounter with your nest-box tenants. Of course, you may encounter issues or challenges that are not covered in this chapter or in this book. I'm constantly learning from my experiences with the birds and from the birds themselves. Reach out to your local or regional community of nest-box landlords for help. You may find just the information and insight you need.

Being a Backyard Landlord

So you want to be a landlord to the birds? It's no accident that the most diligent landlords often have the highest rates for fledging healthy young birds. The good news is that diligence as a bird landlord need not be painful or overly difficult.

Here is an essay by veteran nest-box landlord Julie Zickefoose, who has maintained nest boxes in Connecticut, Maryland, and Ohio over the past three decades.

The Involved Nest-Box Landlord

There are many different approaches to maintaining a nest-box trail. One extreme would be the scout troop that spends a couple of weekends building bluebird boxes, then goes out and mounts those boxes on fenceposts along a country road. After the first year, the young scouts move on with their lives, and if the boxes were ever monitored, they cease to be. The nest boxes go on attracting nesting bluebirds and chickadees, and the local raccoons, rat snakes, mice, and chipmunks key in to that fact, happy to climb the fenceposts and regularly remove and consume each box's birdy contents.

It could legitimately be argued that putting up a box and failing to either protect it from predators or monitor the well-being of the nesting birds is worse than not putting one up at all. When I see an abandoned or neglected nest box trail, I always think of the so-called "ghost traps" that get lost on the sea floor. Lobsters crawl in, attracted to the bait, and eventually die, attracting more lobsters, which crawl in and die, and the dismal cycle continues. An unmonitored, unprotected nest box can attract birds year after year, but nest failures are the rule once predators key in to the box. Monitoring nest boxes at its best is an active pursuit. You have to keep at it to have a good trail. There's an inherent responsibility to the birds you're attracting that, in my view, goes hand in hand with the fun of doing it. Each person will find a comfort level of involvement, but overall I'd strongly recommend starting small and getting a real feel for the work involved before expanding your trail much beyond the number you can realistically monitor on a weekly basis. For me, that's 25 boxes. Of course, not all will be inhabited in a given season, but even a small percentage of that number taking on tenants keeps me hopping!

As a committed nest-box landlord, I have a set of routine maintenance tasks that I carry out weekly on the trail: nest checks, nest changes, and nest-box cleaning. The kit in my car is a small plastic pail that contains a spiral-bound notebook, a ballpoint pen (which won't run in the rain), a screwdriver, a putty knife, and a bag of fresh dry grass, gathered in early spring or just after our hay meadow is cut. I also have a strawberry box lined with paper towels (more on that later). In my notebook, each box I visit is assigned a name. Each time I visit, I mark the date and what I find. I try to hit each box once a week, but no more than that unless there are

NEST BOXES *on unbaffled poles or trees are easily accessed by predators. A raccoon has ripped this box apart.*

KEEPING DATED records of each nest box you visit will help you be an informed, successful landlord.

unusual circumstances, such as cold weather or heavy parasite infestations. I note the amount and type of nesting material, presence of eggs or chicks, presence and type of parasites, such as blowflies or mites, condition of the nestlings, and presence of adult birds. I also make a note of whatever action I took at each nest (usually changing the nest or removing an infertile egg, a wasp nest, or a dead nestling). These notes, which may at first seem trivial, become very useful in keeping track of what's going on in each box. Through your records, you build a profile of each nesting cycle and, over the years, even of the success in each individual box. When you visit your boxes weekly and record what you find, you have instant access to vital information that can come in very handy.

Just as an example of why keeping notes is so important, let's say you open a box and find that a house sparrow has pecked a female bluebird and three four-day-old nestlings to death. Two nestlings cling to life, but it's clear that they are doomed, as the male bluebird will feed, but won't brood nestlings to keep them warm. What to do? If you've kept careful notes, you will know when these nestlings hatched and how old they are. You'll also be able to check your other boxes and see if there are any same-age broods. You just happen to have one a couple of miles away with four four-day-old nestlings. You can take the two survivors and put them in that box, salvaging something from an unpleasant event. This is called cross-fostering, and if you run enough boxes for long enough, you'll find yourself doing it.

By now it may be dawning on you that monitoring and managing bird boxes isn't for the squeamish. I'd highly recommend going out on a sizable nest-box trail with an experienced nest-box landlord before starting your own. This will give you a realistic idea of what you're getting into. Baffling all your boxes against climbing predators will eliminate most of the unpleasant surprises.

Philosophies vary on how much intervention to do. Some trail operators simply clean the box out at the end of the season, not wishing to keep track of what goes on during the nesting season, but I clean the old nest out immediately after each brood fledges, making room for a new nest and subsequent broods.

On trails I've run in Connecticut and southeast Ohio, I've found that blowflies can be a big problem for bluebirds, tree swallows, and chickadees. This bluebottle fly lays its eggs in the nesting material, producing large maggots that suck the nestlings' blood and in large infestations can kill them. The same is true of mites, which in a bad year can infest, weaken, and kill nestlings in many of my boxes. So I routinely check for parasites by slipping a putty knife into the nesting material just below the cup. If I see a damp, dark, and soiled layer, and smell the distinctive funk of blowflies, or if I see minute moving gray specks on the birds, box, and nesting material, I remove the young birds, placing them in a small paper towel–lined strawberry basket for safekeeping. I scrape the infested nest into a bucket, wipe out the box with paper towels, and fashion a new nest by wrapping dry grass around my hand and packing it tightly into the box. Last, I replace the young birds in their new clean nest and dispose of the soiled nest far away from the box.

REPLACING AN infested nest with a clean grass nest.

An involved nest-box landlord watches the weather closely, especially in springtime. Successive days of cold temperatures or rain after young birds have hatched can spell disaster. Both cold and rain will suppress the insect prey the birds need to survive, and box after box of birds can die of starvation after only a day and a half of cold or rain. I've never been fond of having to remove dead nestlings; I'd rather do what it takes to keep them alive. For me, this means feeding starving nestlings in the boxes, then leaving food on the box roof for the adults to give them. I will take a small cooler with a hot water bottle in it from box to box. I'll take the nest with its cold nestlings, and close it in the warm cooler for several minutes until the young are squirming and warm to the touch. Then I whistle softly to the nestlings, and when they gape hungrily, I feed them a scrambled egg and dried fly mixture that I call Bug Omelet. Then I replace them in the box, and using duct tape, affix a jar lid full of the same mixture, with live mealworms too, to the roof of the box. This can be quite an endeavor when you're running 25 boxes and have to visit three times a day. But watching the parent birds flutter down to stuff their bills with food, then feed it to their young, makes it all worthwhile. And opening a box full of fully feathered nestlings with sparkling eyes—that you know would have died without your help—is one of the best feelings in the world.

DURING COLD, inclement weather, some dedicated landlords supplement the food intake of nestling birds with small feedings of scrambled egg.

I've been thinking a lot lately about why I've come to feel such a strong responsibility for the success of the birds using my nest boxes. I think it's because I am, by nature, a highly interventionist nest-box landlord. I'm always peeking in on my tenants, seeing if they need fresh bedding, some parasite control, or perhaps a little supplemental food. So you may take my approach as the opposite extreme from the Saturday scout troop's mount 'em and leave 'em attack.

MALE MOUNTAIN bluebird with food for a nestling.

But another truth that I've discovered is that a nest box is a far more potent attractant to birds than we may realize. It has power, the power to bring a woodland-nesting bird out of the forest and into the middle of a meadow—just witness the woodland chickadees and titmice that come to field-mounted bluebird boxes to nest. These secondary cavity nesters, which lack the tools to excavate their own cavities, are stuck with what nest holes the woodpeckers are done with, and that often means a thoroughly rotten snag, soaked and wet. How much nicer to have a nice, roomy, snug wooden box! A shy chickadee, titmouse, or even a nuthatch may cross an open clearing for a nest site like that.

We put up nest boxes in habitat that looks good to us. But how much do humans really know about what constitutes "good" bluebird, tree swallow, or chickadee habitat? I have boxes scattered over a wide area near my home, and in 20 years of monitoring them I've noticed that one country road consistently produces more and healthier fledglings than the others. There are many factors that likely feed into the equation: frequent mowing schedules for the hayfields; the presence or absence of grazing cattle, which keep the grass desirably short; usable acreage available to the birds; infrequent use of herbicides; even the good quality of the soil beneath the hayfields. Yet bluebirds will consistently return to suboptimal habitat, say in a wooded area, with poorer nesting success, simply because there is an available box there. If you've got a box that consistently fails for one reason or another, consider moving it, or even removing it.

It's no accident that we see more bluebirds around actively mowed lawns, hayfields that are cut several times per season, and grazed pastures. Bluebirds need short grass in order to see their grasshopper, spider, and caterpillar prey. Within the space of a month, a hayfield can go from terrific habitat to practically unusable, where bluebirds are concerned. Similar changes doubtless affect swallows, even though they're aerial insectivores. As a result, my husband, Bill, mows wide circles around all our meadow-mounted boxes, and he takes pains to keep a wide mown path between them. Keeping up with the mowing means the difference between box abandonment and having bluebirds attempt a second or third brood in our meadow.

Box placement and even design can affect nesting success. Consider this story about a nest box in my backyard. I noticed that, several years in succession, I'd lose late bluebird broods in this box to disease. The chicks would suddenly become listless and dehydrated and die, even though the adults were feeding them regularly. I'd remove the corpses as the nestlings would die, and if the bluebirds were lucky they'd raise one or two survivors.

The same thing happened to Carolina chickadees that nested in this box. I stood back and looked at the situation, and it became clear to me what might be going on. Like many bird enthusiasts, I enjoy feeding birds in summer. This bluebird box was on a direct line from the edge of the woods to the feeding station. And I noticed that birds of many species would stop and perch on the box's flat roof on their way to the feeder. And being birds, they'd often defecate before they took off again.

Along comes a bluebird or chickadee parent with a large unwieldy caterpillar or grasshopper. It stops on the nest-box top to subdue and process the prey before feeding its young, removing legs and bashing the prey senseless on the flat box roof—which is covered with the droppings of birds that had stopped there on the way to the feeder. Feces-to-food contact is never a good thing, and in this case it was likely lethal. I disinfected the box with bleach and relocated it to a part of the yard that was not on a direct line to the feeding station, and the nestling deaths stopped. This also caused me to muse about nest-box design—is it possible that a flat box roof, as opposed to a steeply slanted one, is an undesirable thing for precisely this reason?

The more you think about such things, the more you realize that there's a lot more going on in and around nest-box management than it might appear. Monitoring the same trail for a couple of decades tends to throw trends of success and failure into relief. Keeping detailed notes on your birds' nesting success is vital to figuring out what works and what doesn't. And it helps you see just where and when a little intervention can spell the difference between life and death for your tenants. I believe that we, as nest-box landlords, have a responsibility to the birds we attract to protect them from predation, from house sparrow invasion, and from parasites; to keep track of their nesting success, and to do what we can to enhance it. After all, we're luring birds into nesting boxes that are artificial: of human design rather than nature's. We're asking them to build a nest and raise their young in a box sitting right out in the open, where any predator will notice them. If you stop and think about it, we're even making the choice for them of where their territory will lie, the most basic choice a bird can make. Don't we owe it to them to make sure they thrive and prosper in our care? The rewards of being an involved nest-box landlord are counted not just in healthy nestlings, but in the wealth of fascinating encounters and a deep insight into the natural history of the birds we host.

—*Julie Zickefoose, Whipple, Ohio*

A LANDLORD checking a bluebird nest in early spring.

Here are some useful tips for the aspiring nest-box host, designed to enhance your experience as a landlord.

TOP TEN TIPS FOR BACKYARD LANDLORDS

1. CLEAN IN THE SPRING. Early spring is the time to get busy with cleaning out your boxes. In some areas you may find that March or even February is not too early. Sweep all the crud out of the box (making sure it's not this year's nest, of course). If it's still a little grungy, rinse the box with a light bleach-water solution (a capful of bleach in a bucket of warm water), using a scrub brush or an old toothbrush if necessary. Rinse well and let the box air dry before closing the entry. There's no need to place any nesting material inside the box in spring; the birds prefer to do that themselves.

2. MAINTAIN AND REPLACE. Spring is also the time to repair damaged or worn boxes. I take a Leatherman utility tool with me for tightening screws, bending metal baffles back into shape, and pounding loose nails. Sometimes a box is too far gone and must be replaced. This is the perfect time for an upgrade to a better box, a different design, or a box for a different tenant. Read through Chapter 4 for insight into attracting various cavity nesters.

3. PUT THE RIGHT BOX IN THE RIGHT PLACE, AND MAKE SURE IT HAS THE RIGHT HOLE. There are nest boxes that go years without tenants. If you have one of these, your problem could be the box's location. Bluebirds and swallows prefer to use boxes in open grassy areas. House wrens, Carolina wrens, chickadees, titmice, nuthatches, and woodpeckers prefer boxes near or in the woods. Note: When mounting a nest box among trees, make sure there are no overhanging or connecting branches that could provide access from above for snakes, squirrels, mice, or other climbing predators.

   You may also have a box with an improper entry-hole size. The ideal universal entry-hole size is 1½ inches in diameter. This permits entry by most of the smaller birds that use nest cavities. Entries larger than 1½ inches in diameter will permit

A COURTING pair of tree swallows.

European starlings to enter your nest boxes. The appendix has a complete chart of the proper nest-box entry sizes for all cavity-nesting species. Recent studies have indicated that most box-using birds may prefer their boxes to be oriented so that the entrance is facing east.

4. FEND OFF PREDATORS AND PESTS. The onset of nesting is also the start of the nest-predator season. Make sure your boxes are mounted on galvanized metal poles with pole-mounted baffles below the box. Also check to make sure that a predator cannot access the nest box by reaching or jumping from a nearby perch. A thin, 3-inch-long coating of petroleum jelly at the very the base of the pole will discourage in-the-box pests, such as ants, and will be unlikely to come in contact with or affect any other creatures. This must be reapplied after periods of very hot or very wet weather. The same product used very sparingly on the inside roof will discourage wasps and bees from starting nests. Please refrain from using insecticide or pesticides inside your birdhouses. If your boxes are raided by predators during the nesting season, you should do your best to determine which predator gained access to the box and then take steps to prevent a recurrence.

5. KEEP A MONITORING NOTEBOOK. The best way to keep track of your tenants is to keep a watchful eye. Do this by making regular visits to each nest box and recording what you find in your landlord's notebook. A small spiral-bound notebook and a pencil are all you need. Information to record includes name of box (see number 6), date of visit, time of day, weather conditions, contents of the box, number of eggs or young, age and condition of young, presence of adults, presence of parasites, and anything else you can think of that will be a useful reference for future visits. After several years of record keeping you will know and appreciate your most productive boxes and tenants.

6. NUMBER OR NAME THE BOXES. If you have a variety of boxes on your property or an entire trail of boxes (as many bluebird landlords do), it is extremely helpful to name or number and label your boxes. This aids a great deal in record keeping

HOUSE SPARROWS will take over a nest box if given a chance.

LANDLORDS WITH *multiple boxes in a nest-box trail often number their boxes for record-keeping purposes.*

and in helping you remember over the years which boxes are good producers. We've named our nest boxes after their locations on our farm: Upper Meadow box, Spring Trail box, Far Orchard box, etc.

7. ADD OTHER ENHANCEMENTS. Good landlords know there are certain little things you can do to attract the attention of potential tenants. Most cavity-nesting birds prefer an unobstructed path to the entrance, so make sure that vines and brush do not get in the way. Tree and violet-green swallows use white feathers in their nests, so during nest-building time they will readily take a handful of feathers spread across the lawn. Adult bluebirds always seem to appreciate a snag or T-stand (two dowels, small boards, or sticks connected to form a T-shaped perch) that is located 20 to 50 feet from the nest-box entrance. This serves as a song and hunting perch and as a place for fledglings to aim for on their first flight from the box. Great crested flycatchers love a good snakeskin to pull into the nest box. Purple martins readily take to perches above their houses and to trays of crushed eggshells, which they eat for grit and calcium. Barn swallows and robins appreciate a nice puddle of mud for nest construction materials.

8. KNOW YOUR TENANTS. It is important to know which species are using your boxes and how long they incubate their eggs. For instance, the time between incubation and fledging for a bluebird and a tree swallow can differ considerably. Check Chapter 4 for incubation and fledging times of the species nesting in your boxes. Bluebird and purple martin landlords can also rely on the expertise of organizations devoted to these species: the North American Bluebird Society, the Purple Martin Conservation Association, and the Purple Martin Society (see the Resources section for contacts).

9. SCHEDULE YOUR VISITS APPROPRIATELY. If you know the dates of your birds' first eggs and when incubation started, you can guesstimate when to visit safely and when to leave the birds alone (near fledging time). A visit to a box full of 13-day-old bluebirds may cause the nestlings to leave prematurely. If you visit a box and find everyone gone long before the estimated fledging date, you can surmise that the nest met an untimely end. Your familiarity with the birds in your boxes will also help you know when something is not right, such as when you see an agitated adult fluttering near the entry, but intervention is not as good as prevention in the case of predators. In any case, if you find an empty nest, you can clean it out and prepare it for the next potential tenant.

10. COMPARE AND SHARE DATA. As you accumulate more and more data from your nest boxes, you can compare the success of the boxes with each other and with themselves from year to year. You can also share your data with others through online forums such as NestWatch at the Cornell Lab of Ornithology. This kind of data can give you a glimpse into the lives of our most beloved backyard birds—those species that are willing to accept our offerings of housing and shelter. We owe them the helpful stewardship of being good landlords.

TOP TEN PROBLEMS INSIDE THE NEST BOX

You never know what may await you inside each nest box you open. Even boxes with predator baffles, regular monitoring, and diligent parent birds can experience the vagaries of the natural world. Here are a few of the most common problems you may encounter, along with suggested solutions or next steps.

1. NO TENANTS. Some nest boxes simply do not attract any takers. Perhaps the setting is not quite right for a target species. There may be a nesting pair of accipiters (bird-eating hawks) nearby that have made easy meals of prospective

AN EMPTY nest box. If a box remains unused for more than a season, consider moving it to another location.

tenants. Perhaps a wasp or bee nest or marauding ants have kept the house from being used. In the case of accipiters or a wasp or bee nest, moving the box to a different location is wise. For ants, see number 4 in the list of tips for landlords above.

CHICKADEES LINE their nests with soft animal fur, which helps to keep the eggs warm in cold weather.

2. EGGS COLD, NO ADULT. Finding warm eggs in a nest box is a sure sign that incubation is ongoing and the female is still active on the nest. Finding cold eggs means one of two things: the clutch is not completed yet (the female has more eggs to lay) and so the female has not started incubating, or something has happened and the nest has been abandoned. Regardless, it's wise to step away from the box and to watch it from a distance for activity. Try to observe from a place where you are not readily visible to any nearby tenants of the box. If you see no activity, make plans to watch the box at the end of the day or early the next day to see if the adult female returns. Experienced landlords will leave seemingly abandoned nests with cold eggs for two weeks to be absolutely certain they are not being tended. Once you've reached this level of certainty, you can remove the eggs and nest. Poor weather, a predator killing one or both of the nesting adults, or some other disturbance may have caused the abandonment. If you do see the female near the box, she is likely still in the process of laying her clutch. Check back in a few days to chart her progress.

3. EGGS PIERCED OR SMASHED. If the eggs in the box are merely pierced or broken (not missing, chewed up, or removed altogether), your culprit may be another bird, such as a house wren or chickadee, that is trying to take over the box. This often happens to bluebird nests in houses placed too close to woods, thick cover, or buildings—all places where house wrens prefer to nest. Remove the broken eggs and nesting material and move the nest box to an open area far from trees and thick cover. If your egg breaker is a house wren, you may wish to place a wren house at the original site.

4. WEAK NESTLINGS. Several things can cause nestlings to become weak, but the most common are poor weather, which can cause parental abandonment or starvation or hypothermia,

and the debilitating effects of nest mites and blowflies. If, while checking a nest box, you see tiny gray or red specks crawling on your hands, the nest is infested with nest mites. Alternatively, you may notice scabs on the nestlings. This may be a sign of the presence of bluebird blowfly larvae, which live in the nesting material and crawl out at night (when the female can't see to preen them off the young) and suck the blood of nestlings. Use a putty knife to lift the nesting material from the floor of the box. If you see maggots or brown pupal

BLOWFLY LARVAE *look like small, dark pellets. They live in the bottom of nest cavities and can easily be removed.*

capsules, that's a sign that blowfly larvae are present. In both cases, remove the nestlings temporarily to a safe place (we use a small bucket lined with soft tissues), remove and discard the old nest, and sweep the nest box floor clean. Make a new nest from tightly wound and packed dried grass and return the nestlings to their box. Resist the urge to use insecticide inside the nest box. A dash of very hot water on the inside of the box (while the nest is removed) will kill mites. Swabbing the box out with paper towels will remove almost all of them. Then insert your newly made nest, and replace the nestlings in the box. Monitor the box over the next few days to see if the nestlings improve.

5. DEAD NESTLINGS. There are several possible causes of nestling death: starvation or hypothermia from poor weather or parental abandonment; physical attack from a house sparrow, house wren, or other nest-site competitor; parasites or insects; or pesticide contamination. If nestlings are not moving or breathing and are cold to the touch, remove and discard the nest. Observe the box for signs of the parents or of competitor species. When better weather comes, the original pair or a new pair may try again in the box. If you determine that the young were killed by parasites, ants, or insects, it's important to thoroughly wash out the box before allowing it to be reused. Evidence of the presence

of insect pests includes swarming mites inside the box (you'll see and feel them on your hands!) or bite or sting marks on the dead nestlings. Contamination from pesticides is far too common in our lawn-centric neighborhoods. If you treat your lawn with chemicals, either stop this practice or remove your nest boxes. The two really don't coexist well. If your neighbors have the chemical-soaked lawn, consider trying to change their minds.

6. NEST TORN OUT. This is almost certainly evidence of predation by a raccoon. Raccoons are clever predators, excellent climbers, and are able to reach into a nest box with their rather long front arms to grab any birds or eggs. Along with this, they often grab some of the nesting material, which will be scattered about outside the box. At this point it's too late to implement the best possible solution, which is to mount all nest boxes on baffled metal poles.

7. NEST UNDISTURBED, EGGS OR YOUNG GONE TOO SOON. If you've been monitoring your nest box and know when fledging day should be but you find the box empty before that date, something has gone wrong. If there are small sticks placed over the old nest, perhaps a house wren has removed the eggs and is trying to take over the box. The most likely reason, however, is that a snake has consumed the contents of the nest box. Black rat snakes are a nemesis here on our farm. If we did not baffle each one of our boxes, not a single late-spring or summer brood would survive to fledging.

8. DEAD ADULT. If a dead adult has an apparent head wound, it may have been attacked and pecked on the skull by a house sparrow. If there are no apparent physical injuries, it may be chemical poisoning, disease, or starvation that caused the death. Remove dead adults and nestlings and dispose of them safely by burying them or placing them in a trash receptacle.

9. ANTS OR WASPS. Several species of wasps and bees seem to think our nest boxes were erected for their use. The presence of stinging insects inside a nest box can cause nesting birds to

TREE SWALLOWS *can be feisty neighbors.*

abandon a nest or deter them from starting a nest. We carefully remove such pests by squishing them with a flat-sided stick. You can deter them by rubbing a bar of soap on the ceiling of the nest box. In severe cases, a light coating of petroleum jelly also works as a deterrent. For ant infestations, clean out the invaders and coat the base of the mounting pole with a few inches of petroleum jelly.

10. HOSTILE TAKEOVER. In springtime on our farm we see birds fighting and tussling over nest sites. Often we can help resolve this by putting out additional nest boxes to alleviate the pressure. But sometimes we must intervene, especially when house sparrows or starlings are involved. We can deter both of these aggressive nest stealers by consistently harassing them and removing their nests. Sometimes they even take the "You're not welcome!" hint and leave to nest elsewhere. If they don't, many nest-box landlords use in-box traps (the Huber trap is one style) designed to catch birds without harming them. Many organizations for landlords of cavity-nesting birds sell these box traps. See the Resources section at the end of the book.

Not all hostile takeovers are performed by greedy non-native species or aggressively territorial house wrens. Sometimes seemingly gentle, beautiful neighbors just can't seem to get along, as Julie Zickefoose describes in this essay.

When Bluebirds Attack

Using my mad skills of typing without looking at what I'm doing, I sit by the chickadee box in the driveway. It's May 11, 2011, and Phoebe and I, both stricken with strep throat after a busy festival weekend, are at home. It's a crazy warm spring morning and there are warblers dipping through the trees. Bill is taking the *Bird Watcher's Digest* staff birding, so we're down to one pair of binoculars, and we're sharing as we walk slowly down the driveway toward the chickadee box that just yesterday hatched seven perfect pink wrigglers. When I opened the box, seven tiny yellow diamond mouths opened. All four of us crowed with delight, and I took a photo. I didn't know it then, but it would be the last taken of all seven chickadees alive.

Phoebe has the binoculars, and she's excitedly describing birds to me. "Oh! I don't know what this one is! It's got this bright yellow throat, and some black on its face, and a lot of white below . . . Wait! There are two of them, right down low in the pine!" With naked eyes, I see that she's locked onto not one, but two male Blackburnian warblers, not a yard from the ground. I've never been so happy not to be looking through my binoculars. The buzzy *beer beer breee!* of a black-throated blue warbler rings from a hickory tree, and Phoebe gets the male in her sights, all blue, black, and flashy white. It's a great morning.

Finally the driveway chickadee box is in sight, and there is something wrong with the picture. A male bluebird sits on the box, his mate close by. The Carolina chickadees are scolding.

"Oh, Phoebe. This is not good. This is not good. There's something wrong."

Quickly I run to the box, open it, and look inside. As I suspected, the chickadee babies are in big trouble. One is missing. The other six lie on the floor of the box, their nest in disarray. They're cold, pale, lethargic; they haven't been fed or brooded all morning. Massive bruises bloom purple on their tiny heads and backs. I gather them up, lift my shirt, and cradle them against my belly to warm them. How could this have happened? Where did these bluebirds come from? And what has happened to their nest to suddenly make them decide to invade the chickadees' territory?

I dispatch Phoebe to check the nearest box, just a few hundred feet down the driveway. Perhaps something had happened to the nest inside. She opens the box, finds four warm, pipping eggs, and stations herself nearby. Soon the pair

NESTLING EASTERN *bluebirds.*

returns. All is well there. My mind leaps to the bluebird pair about .2 mile down the road. The female abandoned her near-term eggs in a cold spell and never returned. I saw the pair hanging around the box, but the eggs sat unattended, stone cold. Although she was still attended by the male, the female looked to be in poor condition, sitting low on her perch. I figured she just couldn't find enough to feed herself in the cold rain (several days the previous week never got out of the 40s). She couldn't keep the eggs warm, much less feed the babies that were due to hatch in just a few days.

I looked hard at the female bluebird sitting on the chickadee box. She sat low, her fluffed belly feathers covering her feet. Perhaps the pair realized their hayfield territory, grown long, wild, and thick during the rainy spring, wouldn't feed them as well as the sparser grasses along our driveway.

A PAIR of mountain blue-birds atop their nest box.

Having warmed the six chickadee babies back up and replaced them in their box, we drew back into the field to watch. The chickadees warily approached their box, scolding. The moment they tried to enter, the bluebirds swooped down and chased them off. Terrible! We moved closer. The next time it happened, we waved our arms and chased the bluebirds away. The chickadees returned, and one slipped quickly into the box while we held the bluebirds at bay. Good! At least the chicks would be warmed while we figured out what to do next.

I stationed Phoebe near the box and tore down the driveway. Grabbing my garden cart and bucket of bluebird box equipment, I ran out to the yard and pulled up a pole-mounted and baffled bluebird box that had attracted nothing in the last few years. I tossed it into the cart and returned. Eyeballing the situation, I decided to erect it just a few hundred feet from the chickadee box, across the driveway. No sooner had I hammered the post in and topped it with the box than the invading bluebird pair hovered overhead. We ran back into the field as they landed on the new box. Wow! Could it be that easy?

No. It couldn't. The male bluebird was obviously enamored of the new box, but each time he tried to lure his mate over to it, she resolutely returned to the chickadee box. And each time the male chickadee approached his nest box with much-needed food, both bluebirds launched themselves in attack. Horrible. If the chickadees couldn't feed their young, the chicks would never survive.

Phoebe and I put our heads together. What could we do to make the chickadee box less attractive to the bluebirds? Rubber snake, owl decoy? Anything that would scare the bluebirds would scare the chickadees too. "Could we make the hole smaller so the bluebirds couldn't get in but the chickadees could?" Those words came out of my 14-year-old daughter's mouth. I stared at her, open-mouthed. Why hadn't I thought of that? "That's IT!" I exclaimed. "You stay here, make sure those bluebirds don't get back in the chickadee box, and I'll be back."

I ran back to the house, grabbed an empty quart yogurt container, scissors, a compass, some duct tape, and a brown Sharpie marker.

I cut a wide strip of the plastic tub and traced a circle on the reverse, un-printed side. I cut the hole to $1\frac{1}{8}$ inches, which would exclude the bluebirds while admitting the chickadees (bluebirds need a $1\frac{1}{2}$-inch entry hole). Ever the perfectionist, I drew birch-bark dashes on it to match the Gilbertson PVC box.

Filling a syringe with nestling formula and immersing it in a glass of warm water, I headed back out the driveway. By now the female chickadee had been warming her young a good 40 minutes, and they were squirming and more lively. Two had died of massive trauma to their heads and backs. Only four were left now. But they gaped, and I filled them with formula, replaced them in the box, and duct-taped the bluebird excluder over the hole. By now it was about noon. By 1:40 P.M. the chickadees had made several attempts to enter their box, but the smaller hole size gave them pause. And each time they fluttered before the hole, the bluebirds landed on their box and dared them to try to enter.

I moved the lawn chair closer to the box, only about 75 feet away, a distance calculated to discourage the bluebirds while keeping the chickadees comfortable. Four times the chickadees approached bearing food, and four times the bluebirds repulsed them. The bluebirds kept peering inside the box, unable to get any more than their heads inside. Now it was a waiting game. I wanted to see those chickadees go into their box with food. And I wanted to see the bluebirds finally decide to give up on the chickadee box. But I had to feed the chickadee nestlings throughout the whole process, or they'd die. Luckily it was a warm day, around 75 degrees, and the babies would survive being left un-brooded. As long as I warmed them against my skin before feeding them, they were digesting the formula fine and voiding healthy fecal sacs.

Durn bluebirds! I had a garden to plant; lawn to mow, laundry to do, work left untended! Two o'clock came and went, and I continued to warm and feed the baby chickadees every 40 minutes. And each time the adult chickadees approached the box, the blue avengers flared in to drive them away. In between attacks, the bluebirds perched on the new box I'd put up just for them.

I began to reconsider the affection with which I'd always regarded bluebirds: gentle friends to all. Phooey. This pair wanted an already occupied box, and they'd pecked three chicks to death and were clearly bent on starving the rest out. And for their part, I'd had Carolina chickadees repeatedly throw bluebird eggs out of a nest box they coveted. That surprised me too. Watched closely, birds reveal themselves to be quite a bit more cutthroat than we might assume. I thought about Jane Goodall, who watched the Gombe Stream chimpanzee troop for enough hours to record not only tool-using behavior but also infanticide, pre-planned murder, and even skillfully coordinated hunting behavior, with chimps bagging wild pigs and young baboons. They weren't quite the gentle herbivores we'd always imagined them to be.

So this drama unfolded before me. If only the chickadees would accept the bluebird excluder, but they hadn't entered their box since I installed it. Two hours had gone by. The chickadees would return every half-hour with food and would approach the box; the bluebirds would swoop in to defend the box, and the chickadees would eat the food and leave again. It was a race against time. If the chickadees couldn't get in to feed their babies, they might assume after some time that they'd died and abandon them. So I sat by the box, hoping to see the chickadees enter with food; hoping the bluebirds would stick their heads in the reduced hole enough times to realize they were never getting in. Our dog, Chet Baker, lay like an inkblot in the grass, patiently waiting it all out, unwilling to leave my side.

By three o'clock, Phoebe and I were beginning to burn out on box watching. The chickadees appeared with a third bird, and all three perched near the box, scolding. But when one flew down to land there, the bluebirds routed it. The combination of the reduced hole size and the instantaneous bluebird attacks was just too much for the little birds. A new plan began to form in my brain. In our backyard was another Carolina chickadee box, and three of the six eggs had hatched only this morning. I checked again: at 3:30 there were still only three chicks. It was entirely possible that the remaining eggs were infertile. And these four chicks, orphaned by unfortunate circumstance, were only one day older than those three were. I kept the option of fostering the four orphans into the backyard box in my mind's back pocket. That would be a win-win; the back-yard birds could raise a full clutch of seven, and I could finally abandon my post as chickadee guardian and get on with my life!

As I thought about it, these chicks would have all been dead by now, since every attempt their parents had made to feed them today had been thwarted by the bluebirds. It was only the hot weather and my supplemental feedings that had kept them alive until now. Phoebe and I had kept vigilance on the box from 8:30 to 3:30, and not once in that time had the chickadees successfully fed their young. Only twice had a chickadee entered the box, but both events occurred before we put the bluebird excluder on the box. We couldn't remove the blue-bird excluder; the bluebirds would instantly enter the box and kill the remaining chicks.

As the afternoon wore on, Phoebe, Liam, and I watched the little natural events unfolding all around. We found a pair of blue-gray gnatcatchers constructing a nest and watched them tearing blue-green lichens from the branches, then ferrying them up to a sugar maple across the field. A female Baltimore oriole came down to bathe in a driveway puddle, quickly joined by the interloping bluebird pair. A pretty sight, if you forgot what the bluebirds were up to when they weren't bathing. Parula, black-and-white, Blackburnian, Nashville, Tennessee, and Kentucky warblers sang all around. A red-eyed vireo foraged in the maples around the box. A white-eyed vireo landed on a branch just over Liam's head, voiced one funny sputtery song, then flew low over his head, making him chuckle. Both yellow-billed and black-billed cuckoos voiced their mellow songs on either side of us. We'd all learned something about bluebirds we'd never known before, and we'd figured out how to keep four two-day-old chickadees alive and well while their besieged parents dithered helplessly.

"See, Phoebe, this is what it would be like to be a field ornithologist. Think you'd want to do that?" She gave me a quizzical look. "I dunno. How does it pay?" I chuckled. "Well, you'd probably have to be in a teaching position at a university, and you'd spend your summers doing this." I could see her processing that in her mind, the same mind that had come up with the idea of the bluebird excluder, that had registered its first Blackburnian and black-throated blue warblers only this morning. At 14, she's had more exposure to beautiful birds and fascinating days like this one than I'd had by the time I was 25. I can't wait to see what comes of all this, what she becomes. One thing I'm sure of: she cares, is completely engaged, and she's willing to put in the time and effort to stop and help.

At 4:20 I packed it in, loaded the lawn chairs and thermos, the binoculars and cameras and laptop and snacks into the garden cart. I fed the babies one last time and cradled their box in my arm as I pulled my equipment up the driveway. I called Phoebe and Liam to help me put them in the backyard box. The four orphans squirmed down next to the three hatchlings and three eggs. One chickadee parent entered the box and didn't come back out. Another flew in and stayed for five minutes, then left, presumably to forage for their suddenly expanded family. With luck, they'd all grow up to be wild chickadees, raised by foster chickadee parents. That was much to be preferred to being raised by a human, and infinitely better than dying of starvation and exposure. It had been an odd day, a good day, a day well spent.

—*Julie Zickefoose, Whipple, Ohio*

UNWANTED TENANTS

Some nest-box landlords are interested in hosting only certain birds — sometimes only a single species. While I admire their devotion to their purple martins or bluebirds or wood ducks, I find it hard to understand that some of these otherwise kind-hearted folks actually throw out the nests of any bird that uses their nest boxes that is not their intended tenant, including tree swallows and great crested flycatchers!

I'm more of a generalist, I guess. I just want to help any cavity-nesting species that honors me with its presence in one of our nest boxes. If we put out a nest box for eastern bluebirds only to have tree swallows take it over, we put up another box 25 or so feet away, and — usually — the neighbors get along. After all, it's a tough old world out there, especially for species that cannot excavate their own nest cavities. So the only unwanted tenant advice I'm going to give is for handling house sparrows and European starlings. Here's my advice: throw them out. Make it difficult for them

FEW SERIOUS landlords permit house sparrows to nest in boxes intended for native songbirds.

to use your boxes. If all else fails, remove your housing until these cavity hogs leave for greener pastures. Some landlords capture and relocate or destroy starlings and house sparrows. For advice on how to do that, contact one of the organizations listed in the Resources section.

HOUSE SPARROWS

If you live near a colony of nesting house sparrows and you put up nest boxes, you will be confronted with this hardheaded species. House sparrows love a large, dark cavity, so nest-box designs that use slot-shaped entrances (which admit much more light than circular entrances) or are built from white PVC pipe are too bright inside for the sparrows' liking. Placing nest boxes far from human habitation, either in wide-open spaces or well inside a wooded area, will also deter house sparrows.

EUROPEAN STARLINGS

This aggressive nest grabber uses its long, sharp bill to jab at other cavity-nesting species, in an attempt to drive them away from a contested nest site. There's nothing more disappointing than seeing a

native bird driven from its nest site by an aggressive pair of starlings. Nest boxes with an entrance hole smaller than 1 9/16 inches in diameter will prevent starlings from entering. Purple martin landlords have devised some strategies to discourage starlings, including the use of natural or plastic nesting gourds, which sway in the wind (starlings dislike this), and the use of crescent-shaped entrance holes that martins can use but starlings cannot.

Frequently Asked Questions

Q: *If I check a nest box, will I scare the birds away? Will my human scent drive off the parents?*

A: If you've been monitoring your nest boxes, you should know the approximate stage of progress for the nest. Knowing the hatching day is most useful. It's perfectly fine to look inside a nest box up until about 10 days after hatching, because the nestlings are not yet ready to leave the nest. After 12 days, it's best to watch the nest from a distance because the young birds are close to fledging and any sudden disturbance, such as your opening the box, might cause a panicked departure.

Birds do have a sense of smell, but much remains to be learned about how well developed it is, particularly in passerines. A parent bird's instinct to care for its young is going to far outweigh any slight disturbance caused by your visiting the nest box. The more likely scenario is that a snake or a raccoon will follow your scent trail to the nest. For this reason, I always recommend that nest boxes be placed on baffled metal poles to prevent predation.

Q: *Can a single parent raise the nestlings?*

A: It is possible, and we've witnessed it on our farm with bluebirds and tree swallows, but it's far from ideal. Nests that lose one adult have a better chance of success if the loss happens close to fledging time. Many adult male birds do not participate at all in incubation or brooding. If a female is killed, the male is unable to incubate eggs or brood the young in her place. If the male is killed, the female may not be able to incubate the eggs or brood the young and forage for herself and the nestlings. The typical result of the loss of one or the other of a mated pair of cavity-nesting birds is a failed nesting attempt.

Q: *How long do the parents care for the nestlings?*

A: The time between hatching from the egg and fledging from the nest varies widely among cavity-nesting birds. Young barn owls spend almost two months in the nest, whereas young wood ducks leap from the nest at the ripe old age of one day. General nestling development information is in Chapter 4. For most songbirds, the time from hatching to fledging is about 10 to 14 days. Cup-nesting birds tend to fledge sooner, whereas cavity-nesting species, being in a more protected setting, develop more slowly. But for all cavity-nesting birds, the parental care continues for weeks after fledging day. Many recently fledged birds continue to receive feedings, parental protection, and attention for weeks after leaving the nest.

Q: *Should I leave my nest boxes up all winter?*

A: Yes. Nest boxes provide valuable roosting sites for many birds in winter. We always get downy woodpeckers roosting in our nest boxes—a species that has never actually nested in them. If the winters are cold where you live, you may consider doing a few things to make the inside of the boxes more comfortable for the birds. Using flexible weather stripping, plug the vent holes to reduce the draft of cold air and increase the retention of body heat inside the nest box. Place a few inches of dried grass or wood chips on the bottom of the box for additional insulation and comfort.

IN WINTER, nest boxes may be used for roosting by former tenants or other species.

Q: *Should I clean out last year's old nest?*

A: This is a topic of some debate among nest-box researchers. Messy, droppings-covered old nests should definitely be removed for health reasons. Some researchers believe that a bit of nesting material inside a box enhances its attractiveness to prospecting pairs of birds. Others claim that nest building is

A NEST box with a predator baffle in place.

an important part of the courtship and breeding process and so we should allow our tenants to build their own nests. We split the difference on our boxes. If the old nest is clean and well built, and it looks like the nesting pair may have a second brood, we leave the nest. However, if the nest is soiled or even a little bit gross, we remove it, brush out the box to remove bug bits, poop, and discarded feathers and feather sheaths, and let the birds start from scratch.

Q: *Do I really need to baffle my nest boxes?*

A: If you've read any of the preceding chapters, you know I'm going to say yes! The places I've lived and put out nest boxes have all had high numbers of nest-box predators, so any unbaffled boxes were very vulnerable. However, if you know you do not have nest-box predators in your area (and I'm not exactly sure where that might be), go ahead and try it. Just expect me to say "I warned you!" when you open up a nest box to find that a predator has visited. Baffles require a bit of extra work, but I'd rather do that work than find that some of my "babies" have been eaten by a hungry rat snake or raccoon.

Q: *Why are there no tenants in my boxes?*

A: There are many reasons why a nest box might not be used. It could be in a poor location that makes birds feel unsafe, such as near a busy road or doorway. The entry hole might be too small to permit your local cavity nesters to enter. Perhaps the box itself is not built to the proper specifications. Or there may be a nearby predator that keeps birds from feeling safe about using your box. If the housing specifications are correct, try moving the box to a different location and watch to see if there's any increased interest.

Q: *What's the best material for building a nest box?*

A: Most nest boxes are made from wood. Wood that weathers well, such as cedar, is best. Pine is cheap and easy to get, but it cracks easily if it is not sealed and stained or painted. Hardwoods such as oak, walnut, and cherry also tend to dry out and to warp. A material that is being used increasingly is PVC pipe. It stands up to weather very well and is lightweight. Plywood might seem like a good wood to use for building nest boxes, but it tends to fall apart after a season or two of harsh weather.

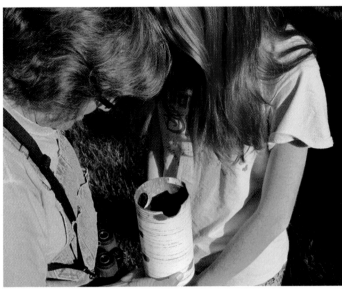

A NEST box made from PVC pipe.

Q: *Can I paint my nest boxes?*

A: Yes. Painting or staining on the outside will help your nest boxes last longer by protecting the wood from sun and moisture. Lighter colors deflect the heat of strong sunlight in summer. Boxes placed in shaded habitat can be painted any color, as long as it does not make the house more visible to predators. Many nest-box authorities (and I concur) discourage painting the inside of nest boxes. Paint or stain can be toxic to featherless nestlings, which come into regular contact with the inside walls of a nest box.

Q: *Can I use pesticides to get rid of mites?*

A: No. The use of any chemical inside a nest box is a bad thing. If you find a nest box that's infested with mites, lice, blowflies, or some other pest, remove the nestlings and place them in a temporary nest (a bowl lined with tissues works). Remove the infested nest and replace it with a nest cup made from fresh, clean materials, then replace the nestlings. In the case of mites, dash some hot water in the empty box and swab it out with a paper towel, then replace the nesting material with tightly packed dried grass formed into a nest cup. Check on the nestlings in a day or two to see if they look better. Featherless nestlings absorb chemicals through their skin, and they are highly sensitive to chemical poisoning. When nestlings do come in contact with pesticides, the result is often tragic.

ACORN WOODPECKERS *(this one's a male) create huge caches of acorns and other nuts by drilling small storage holes at a single site.*

Q: *A woodpecker is drilling a hole in the wooden siding of my house. How do I make it stop?*

A: There is no way to be certain why a woodpecker drills holes in the wooden siding of a house, but we have plenty of hypotheses. First of all, to a woodpecker, a dark, wood-sided home in the woods may simply appear to be a giant tree. Some woodpeckers just like to make noise by hammering on metal eave spouts and chimney flues. This type of territorial drumming rarely causes any damage, except perhaps to your eardrums. When a woodpecker drills a single large hole, it may be trying to excavate a nesting cavity. Assuming you do not want this, I suggest you place metal flashing over the hole and see if this forces the bird to seek a home site elsewhere. If this does not work, and the bird simply moves to the side of the flashing and starts again, try scaring the bird away using loud noises, a squirt from the garden hose, or even rubber snakes hung near the site—all of which have worked as deterrents. If you'd like to have a woodpecker nesting in close proximity to you, consider placing an appropriately sized nest box over the damaged site. Fill the box with wood chips (woodpeckers prefer to excavate when choosing a nest site). The birds may take advantage of this convenient nest site.

If the woodpecker is drilling multiple small holes, it may be trying to excavate food, such as termites or carpenter ants. If you are certain your siding does not host either of these pests, perhaps the woodpecker is hearing the humming and buzzing of electrical appliances inside your house and thinks it is a busy colony of fat, juicy termites. Use the same scare-away techniques suggested above. In extreme circumstances, if all else fails, contact your local wildlife official to come and remove the offending bird.

Q: *I've noticed bites eaten out of my garden veggies and fruits. Who is doing this?*

A: House finches, cardinals, sparrows, and a variety of other backyard birds are known to sample the fruits and vegetables from our gardens. It's a common occurrence, but it rarely destroys the entire crop. Mesh crop netting surrounding your garden plants will eliminate the birds' access. I've used a plastic owl and a homemade human scarecrow to keep birds out of the vegetable garden. Both worked for a short while, then the birds resumed their assault. Some of the more philosophical gardeners simply plan to grow enough to go around!

Q: *I've noticed house sparrows eating the mortar from between the bricks at my neighbor's house. What's up with that?*

A: Seed- and insect-eating birds need a certain amount of "grit" to help them digest their "hard" foods. Bits of grit, such as the sand in mortar, are stored in a bird's gizzard, where they work to grind hard foods down into small pieces. In winter, birds such as evening grosbeaks and crossbills can frequently be seen along roadsides where they are consuming bits of cinder and road salt for the same reason. Don't worry. It's unlikely the sparrows will tear down your neighbor's house (unless the woodpeckers help them out . . .).

Q: *I found a dead bird in my yard/nest box. What do I do with it?*

A: The easiest and safest thing is to dispose of the bird by burying it or throwing it in the trash. Although humans are not in immediate danger from avian disease transmission from dead birds, it's wise to be cautious. Handle dead birds with gloves or plastic bags on your hands. Some scientific institutions and natural history or university museums welcome donations of dead birds for their collections and research. If you find a dead bird that is recently deceased (such as a window strike) and you know a local institution that accepts "salvage" birds, save the bird in a sealable plastic bag and place it in your freezer until you can donate it. Always document the date, location, and cause of death and write this in waterproof ink on a slip of paper inside the bag with the bird. Please note: it is illegal to possess a native or migratory bird without holding special permits. If you cannot find an institution that accepts donations of dead birds, it's best to dispose of the carcasses properly.

FREE-ROAMING HOUSE-CATS *and feral cats kill millions of songbirds annually.*

Q: *I've lost several birds to outdoor cats. How do I keep cats away from my bird feeders and nest boxes?*

A: Free-roaming cats kill millions of birds each year. If it's your pet doing the killing or injuring of birds, consider keeping it indoors, where it's safe from disease, busy streets, and encounters with stray animals and predators. If it's a neighbor's cat, ask them to restrain it. If this does not work, and the cat is still attacking birds in your yard, you may need to try something a bit more creative. Catch the cat in a live trap and return it to the neighbor with a further request that it not be allowed to roam. If the problem persists, you can always recapture the cat and take it to the local humane society. Or if this seems too harsh, fill a super soaker squirt gun with a 50/50 blend of water and white vinegar. Give the cat a blast with this stinky concoction. Cats dislike getting wet, and they will dislike the taste of this when they try to lick themselves dry. The owner should get the message too.

Q: *There's a hawk watching the birds at my feeder. How do I scare it away?*

A: Bird-eating hawks are a natural part of the ecosystem. They weed out weak, slow, and naive individuals, which helps keep our wild bird populations healthy. Both sharp-shinned and Cooper's hawks are attracted by the bird activity at our feeding stations and nest boxes, and they occasionally catch, kill, and consume the birds we work so hard to attract. Try to enjoy the presence of a hawk for the natural role it plays in nature. If you just can't stand the idea of a hawk eating one of your backyard birds, step outside and let the hawk see you. Hawks are typically shy and will fly away once you open your door or window. If the problem persists, stop feeding birds for a week or two. When the bountiful food supply (your feeder birds) is dispersed, the hawk will seek its sustenance elsewhere.

Q: *Every night the deer come into my yard and empty my feeders. What can I do?*

A: The only real solution is to bring your feeders inside at night. Hungry deer rearing up on their hind legs can reach surprisingly high to get at your feeders—probably higher than you can

ACCIPITERS SUCH as sharp–shinned (shown) and Cooper's hawks are aerial predators that specialize in songbird prey. They often key in to activity at bird feeders.

hang them. I've tried all manner of deer repellents to keep our local white-tailed deer away from our feeders and flower beds. Nothing worked until we got a dog that likes to patrol the yard at dusk. Our dog, Chet, would spook the deer away nightly until they chose not to visit the feeders anymore. Another option is to install fencing around the feeding station and favorite plantings. Our vegetable garden is surrounded by a 9-foot-high plastic mesh fence. Most feeders are raided by hungry, climbing raccoons. You can stop this plundering by hanging your feeders from metal poles that have a metal predator baffle mounted high, under the feeders. This will prevent the raccoons from gaining access to feeders, just as it protects your nest boxes.

Chapter 6: The Birdy Backyard All-Stars

SOME OF THE WORLD'S GREATEST IDEAS have come from a moment of inspiration or from seeing a version of a great idea realized by someone else. In the world of writing, this sort of idea grabbing might be considered plagiarism. In the realm of bird gardening, great ideas grow like the fruits on a blackberry bush and we are free to pluck them for ourselves. In the spirit of drawing inspiration from another's effort, this chapter profiles several bird gardeners from across North America. I'm calling these folks the Birdy Backyard All-Stars because each one of them has devoted a lot of time and effort to turning their property into bird-friendly habitat.

These backyards are scattered all across the U.S. and come in all shapes, sizes, and settings—from small suburban plots to large pieces of rural acreage. I've noted which USDA Plant Hardiness Zone each backyard is in, as this information is invaluable when selecting which plants to grow. I've surveyed and interviewed the all-stars to gain some insight into their birds of bird paradise. Here's what each of them has to share with you.

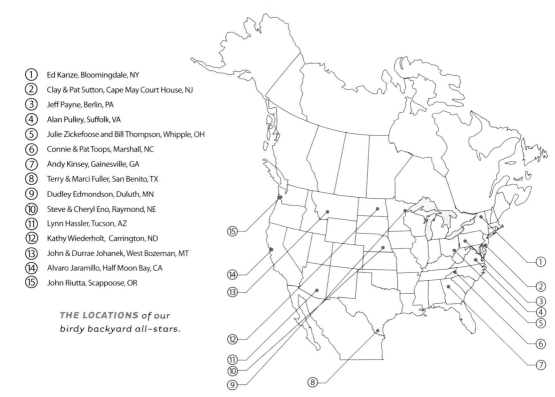

1. Ed Kanze, Bloomingdale, NY
2. Clay & Pat Sutton, Cape May Court House, NJ
3. Jeff Payne, Berlin, PA
4. Alan Pulley, Suffolk, VA
5. Julie Zickefoose and Bill Thompson, Whipple, OH
6. Connie & Pat Toops, Marshall, NC
7. Andy Kinsey, Gainesville, GA
8. Terry & Marci Fuller, San Benito, TX
9. Dudley Edmondson, Duluth, MN
10. Steve & Cheryl Eno, Raymond, NE
11. Lynn Hassler, Tucson, AZ
12. Kathy Wiederholt, Carrington, ND
13. John & Durrae Johanek, West Bozeman, MT
14. Alvaro Jaramillo, Half Moon Bay, CA
15. John Riutta, Scappoose, OR

THE LOCATIONS of our birdy backyard all-stars.

Ed Kanze

Bloomingdale, New York

USDA ZONE 3

<NESTLED ALONG A RIVERBANK> in New York's 6-million-acre Adirondack Park is the backyard of long-time naturalist and bird watcher Ed Kanze. Ed, his wife, Debbie, and their two children love their bit of mountain paradise and all the nature that lives right outside their door, including moose, black bears, gray jays, and a host of warblers during the spring and summer.

When Ed and Debbie first moved to this location in 2000, the property consisted of perfectly manicured lawns with scores of flowering hydrangea bushes. Ed immediately set to work—retiring the John Deere lawn tractor that came with the place and letting the surrounding "lawn" grow to a more natural state. The result: 3 or 4 acres of naturally occurring goldenrod meadows sloping down to the river.

Ed writes: "We love living here, although it's a tough sort of love at times, given all the biting insects. We have blackflies in plague proportions from early May until early July. It's a price we pay for living on the banks of a clear-flowing, highly oxygenated stream in the North Woods, where blackfly larvae in the mucky bottom serve as the prime detritivores. We also have mosquitoes in astounding numbers, deerflies, and no-see-ums that make it impossible to have a light on at night near an open window. Although we hate to admit it, retiring our lawn and turning it into a wildflower meadow had one negative consequence amidst the legion of positives: it created a moist habitat near the ground where mosquitoes find refuge during the heat of the day.

"And so, while making our place birdier, and by making it far more friendly to garter snakes, meadow voles, and grass spiders, we've also made it more buggy. But that's life, I guess. Every gain requires a trade-off. We've gladly made ours and we stick by it. Very little mowing and very many birds, including the cedar waxwings that arrive like clockwork every June to harvest wild strawberries from our ex-lawn before we can get to them."

Because of the extreme winters in this region (often hitting -40 degrees F), many things will not grow here, but the natural habitat that the Kanzes allow to flourish on their property serves as a haven for birds and wildlife. The spruce-balsam woods bring in ruffed grouse and winter wrens; the open meadows accommodate eastern bluebirds

ED KANZE.

THE KANZE *family's house and yard.*

and chipping sparrows; and the riverbanks and swamps attract great blue herons, American bitterns, belted kingfishers, and numerous waterfowl. The Kanzes have witnessed some unusual birds in their backyard habitat, including an eastern towhee that developed the ability to mimic the vocalizations of blue jays. This towhee's unique vocal talent has been recorded and archived at the Cornell Lab of Ornithology.

As Ed's property demonstrates, sometimes the best thing you can do to create good bird habitat is to do nothing. "Let the grass grow," says Ed. "Let the milkweed and goldenrod flourish along with the bugs, spiders, and garter snakes. The birds will thank you for it."

Their family has grown with the addition of children, and as the kids have grown, the Kanzes have enjoyed sharing their passion for the natural world with daughter Tasman and son Ned. One of their more intriguing nature projects is a bio-survey in which they attempt to identify and catalog every living creature on their property.

Ed describes the bio-survey. "We started it as soon as we stepped onto this piece of land, and now the kids are really into working on it too. We look at everything, from mammals and birds and trees, to mosses and insects and spiders. It's really fun and a good excuse to spend time outside. We really want to learn what's living here with us so we can do a better job of improving the property for all concerned. We're not high-tech about it at all—we keep the records on index cards. I counted them the other day and we're somewhere around 500 different species identified and cataloged for our place. We're working on moths currently and having a blast!"

Ed sums up his bird gardening this way: "Lots of things in the world seem to be getting worse. It's a source of comfort and satisfaction to look out on our riverside acres in the Adirondack Mountains and see a place that grows more wild and beautiful every year."

Clay and Pat Sutton

Cape May Court House, New Jersey

USDA ZONE 7A

CLAY AND PAT SUTTON's birdy backyard is in southern New Jersey, about 12 miles north of Cape May. They bought their home in 1977 and have spent the past 35 years restoring the house and improving the gardens. Their property is just under a ½ acre of former farmland—in fact it was originally part of a farm owned by Clay's great-grandfather. Clay and Pat live in an old house that was built in 1845 and was moved to the site in the mid-1950s. About a third of their land is a woodlot that's approximately 50 years old. Another third is a perennial flower garden, and the remaining third includes the house, a tiny front yard, and a small meadow.

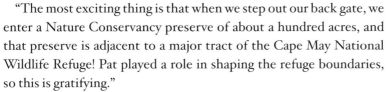
PAT SUTTON in her perennial garden.

They describe the setting of their property this way: "We live on the outskirts of a rural farmland community that has somehow managed to survive on the edge of a tourist-driven seashore area. There are still a number of active small farms around us. We are adjacent to lowland swamp forest and pine-oak upland woodlands. We are only a quarter-mile from a Delaware Bay tributary stream, one-half mile from Delaware Bay salt marsh, and about two miles from the Delaware Bay. On a quiet night, we can hear rails from the backyard, and we enjoy flyover shorebirds and wading birds daily.

THE SUTTONS' backyard when they purchased the property.

"The most exciting thing is that when we step out our back gate, we enter a Nature Conservancy preserve of about a hundred acres, and that preserve is adjacent to a major tract of the Cape May National Wildlife Refuge! Pat played a role in shaping the refuge boundaries, so this is gratifying."

When the Suttons moved in, the former owner bragged how he'd bulldozed the property bare, except for the small woodlot, which was spared only because the bulldozer broke down. That first summer they did not mow the property at all, curious to see what plants would "volunteer." Among these were an American holly and a dwarf hackberry, both of which have now grown taller than 50 feet.

THE SAME backyard today.

BUSY FEEDERS at the Suttons' place.

Over the past three decades the Suttons have created a small meadow and planted native trees, shrubs, perennial gardens, and caterpillar food plants. They've also come up with a natural-looking solution to maintaining the privacy of their backyard, which has neighbors close on each side: "We have encouraged living fences to separate our habitat from our manicured neighbors' properties on either side. Our living fence, which is more of a hedgerow today, began as a chainlink fence to contain two rambunctious English setters. We let weeds and vines consume the fence, and today our oasis is hidden by a wall of vegetation, despite neighbors on both sides cutting back and herbiciding their side of our fence. It is a privacy fence—for us and the birds—but also provides all-important shelter for birds and a safe corridor to the feeding stations."

They also maintain two large brush piles for the birds to use as shelter, and several water features—misters, drippers, ponds, and birdbaths—that attract and benefit birds, dragonflies, frogs, toads, and turtles. Eastern screech-owls have nested in boxes the Suttons have placed in the woods and yard.

The birds, bees, and butterflies seem to be most attracted to the Suttons' perennial gardens: "We don't deadhead the perennials, and as soon as things begin to go to seed, birds start feasting. Many insect-eating birds are attracted to the perennial garden. Come winter we leave it standing, and the cover and seed heads attract birds all winter long. We buy bird seed and keep our feeding station going, but often the hotspot is the still-standing perennial garden."

Their own favorite feature of the yard is the tiny woodland, which by 2007 had grown into a tangle of invasive Japanese honeysuckle

and multiflora rose. They hired a young landscaper to remove the exotic jumble using a brush hog mower, but not until they had carefully flagged all the native trees, shrubs, and dead snags they wished to preserve. They fenced the woodlot to keep the white-tailed deer from eating all the precious saplings, shrubs, grasses, and wildflowers, and today the habitat is like a native tree nursery with hundreds of black cherry, persimmon, sassafras, oak, red cedar, dwarf hackberry, and sweet gum trees.

"Every year we pot up dozens of these seedlings to share with fellow wildlife gardeners. We've complemented the woodlot with additional favorites like sweetbay magnolia, mountain laurel, and New Jersey tea. Our woodlot functions as a huge bird feeder. It produces a supermarket full of fruits, seeds, and caterpillars (and other insects), all because it is a healthy woodlot of native plants."

In addition to sharing their plants with bird-gardening friends, the Suttons also share their expertise. Pat has taught a series of workshops—"Backyard Habitat for Birds, Butterflies, Dragonflies, and More"—for the last 30 years, and she has led "Tours of Private Wildlife Gardens" for the past 21 years (and continues to do so). Legions of wildlife gardeners have sprouted from these learning experiences.

The greatest challenges the Suttons face are invasive plants and living in a tourist-based area where many properties are rentals, meaning lots of manicured lawns drenched in lawn-care chemicals. Clay and Pat continue to do their part to help their neighbors near and far do a better job of providing for birds and wildlife.

Clearly the Suttons' efforts at making a bird-friendly yard have been noticed by the birds. Their yard bird list (including flyovers) is 213 species! Highlights include overwintering black-headed and rose-breasted grosbeaks, a male varied thrush, and one memorable fall day when they enjoyed 31 warblers of 11 species feeding in their yard all day. Winter holds some great memories too, including 18 northern cardinals and 119 white-throated sparrows in sight at one time at the feeding stations, brush piles, and water features. But it's not just birds that are attracted to this birdy corner of the Garden State. The 76 butterfly species Clay and Pat have identified on their property constitute the second-highest total for a single yard in New Jersey!

THE WOODLOT before the removal of invasive plants.

AFTER THE removal of the invasive plants.

THE SAME woodlot all grown up in native plants.

Jeff Payne

Berlin, Pennsylvania

USDA ZONE 4

JEFF LOVES *birding around the pond's edge habitat.*

JEFF PAYNE'S home was a family farm before he owned it. This photo was taken circa 1949.

JEFF PAYNE MOVED TO BERLIN, Pennsylvania, to begin his practice as a veterinarian more than 20 years ago. He and his wife, Retta, also a veterinarian, found an old 37-acre farm atop the Allegheny Mountains. It was almost perfect for this pair of avid birders, with 12 acres of open hay meadow and about 25 acres of mixed woods containing oak, maple, ash, and cherry trees, among other species.

A closer look revealed soils that were worn out from decades of subsistence farming and field edges that were kept a bit too tidy to benefit birds and wildlife. They also faced the challenge of being in a cold microclimate on their ridgetop, at an elevation of just under 3,000 feet. This meant that their weather was often 10 degrees colder than in the surrounding valleys.

They immediately set about making improvements to make the farm more bird-friendly. They added a ½-acre pond with wetland edges in 1991. This quickly became a favorite feature of the property, attracting migrating waterfowl, nesting mallards and wood ducks, and visits from passing shorebirds and even an American bittern.

With regular applications of lime and organic fertilizer, Jeff and Retta developed an acre of ground as a wildlife feeding area. They planted another plot in warm-season native grasses, such as switchgrass and big bluestem, with scattered clumps of native wildflowers (purple coneflower, coreopsis, sunflowers). They allowed these areas to grow until they bloomed or produced seed, then mowed them intermittently to keep the habitat as open field.

The fencerows were another matter, which Jeff describes: "We allowed the fencerows to grow up naturally and augmented their progress a bit with some native plantings. What came up naturally was mostly native volunteers: arrowwood viburnum, blackberry, serviceberry, and hawthorn. We managed other areas of the fencerows to keep them at an early-succession stage of growth—removing fast-growing trees and all the non-natives we could control."

These fencerows are now the birdiest parts of the property, used by nesting birds in the breeding season and as foraging and resting habitat by myriad vireos, warblers, tanagers, orioles, and thrushes during both spring and fall migration. Their location south of the pond is visible from the back deck of the house, making a perfect set-up for birding.

Also encouraged to grow on the property are large patches of blackberry. These provide summer fruits for both the Paynes and their wild neighbors, and the thorny canes are excellent escape and roosting cover for birds year-round. "And for great pies and jam!" Jeff adds.

Among the unusual species recorded on the Paynes' property are two records of rufous hummingbird (in 1996 and 2009), a short-eared owl, and semiannual records of Connecticut warbler. Their yard list stands at an astounding 197 bird species!

Asked if he'd like to have a do-over on any of the bird gardening he has done, Jeff was quick to reply: "I wouldn't plant any nursery stock for wildlife. Instead, I'd encourage native plants to grow on the property—with a special focus on the ones with the greatest wildlife value. The couple of non-natives that we did not remove in the early years are now pests, especially crown vetch and yellow water iris."

His advice to bird gardeners in the Northeast: "Be patient. Work with the plants and features that nature provides. Create as much diverse habitat as possible. Keep a journal and have fun!"

TWO VIEWS of the pond on Payne Mountain.

Alan Pulley

Suffolk, Virginia

USDA ZONE 8A

ALAN PULLEY.

LOCATED ABOUT 35 MILES from the ocean, and close to the North Carolina line, Suffolk, Virginia, is the home of Alan Pulley and his family. Like many first-time homeowners, the Pulleys purchased a house in a relatively new subdivision in a rural-suburban setting. The land had been farmed before being developed into a subdivision about a decade ago. The topography is flat, and the soil is mostly fine, sandy topsoil. Nearby wooded patches bordering a lake include oak, birch, maple, cherry, poplar, beech, pine, and sweet gum trees.

"There was very little established flora on our property in 2006 when we moved in—the property was about 95 percent lawn," Alan said. "There were a few foundation shrubs around the house, one small flower bed in the front yard, and three small trees scattered throughout the landscape—and that's it. The previous owners did very little to the landscape outside of caring for the lawn. I liked the fact that I was basically starting with a blank slate, but I knew that there would be challenges gardening in sandy soil in full sun. I still have lots of lawn to eliminate but feel like I've made great progress in six years."

One of the first things Alan added to the landscape after moving in was a bird feeder, and Ameri-

ALAN PULLEY'S front yard when his family moved in.

THE PULLEYS' front yard after some bird-friendly improvements.

can goldfinches were his first customers. He now maintains a few feeding stations in the yard along with a large birdbath. He's added various, mostly native, plants—both coniferous and deciduous—for food as well as shelter for the birds. Some of the plantings include a willow oak, serviceberries, river birches, witch hazel, several hollies, and various vines and perennials. Each spring Alan grows a patch of annual sunflowers for the finches, and he leaves them standing throughout the fall and winter. Another popular winter hangout for the birds is a large brush pile that Alan makes each fall from pruned limbs and shrub clippings. Cavity nesters, including eastern bluebirds, Carolina chickadees, tree swallows, and purple martins, use the birdhouses throughout the yard.

Among Alan's favorite features of his bird-friendly property are the large open areas where the bluebirds, tree swallows, and purple martins nest. A nearby lake provides lots of great looks at birds flying to and from the water, including bald eagle, osprey, herons and egrets, and ducks and geese. But most of the birds that Alan enjoys on his property are those that prefer the feeders, birdbath, and the native coral honeysuckle vines growing along the deck.

"The coral honeysuckle is a favorite among the hummingbirds," he says. "In the fall the mockingbirds and robins feed on the berries. Chickadees often forage for

THE PULLEYS' backyard before they improved it.

THE PULLEYS' backyard now.

THE BIRDBATH before and after habitat improvements.

ALAN HAS help from his daughter in improving the backyard habitat.

WINTERBERRY IS one of the bird-friendly plants that Alan Pulley has added to his yard.

A CHIPPING sparrow nest in Alan Pulley's yard.

insects in the tangled interior of the vines. We even had a northern mockingbird nest in it this spring!"

While the list of birds that Alan has seen in or from his yard is a respectable 78 species, he's adding new ones with some regularity, including red-headed woodpecker this past spring and common redpoll in the winter of 2010.

As his bird list and enjoyment grow, so does Alan's hunger for knowledge about gardening for birds. He recently became certified as a master gardener, which helped him recall one of his only regrets about the improvements he's made to his property. "I've learned so much about gardening and birds over the past six years. It's been wonderful. My only slight regret would be some of the plant choices that I made early on. I added some non-native plants that were invasive and wanted to take over the backyard. They're gone now, but I learned my lesson. It's important to do a little research prior to buying a particular plant if you don't know much about it. And if you're gardening for the birds, go native whenever possible."

In the future Alan hopes to add a garden pond, some tree snags, a chimney swift tower, and of course, more plants to his increasingly bird-friendly habitat.

Julie Zickefoose and Bill Thompson

Whipple, Ohio

USDA ZONE 6

TWO VIEWS *of the Zickefoose–Thompson homestead in its first year under their ownership.*

JULIE ZICKEFOOSE AND I moved onto our 40-acre old farmstead in southeastern Ohio in late 1992. A few years later we bought the adjoining 40 acres of woodland. Our 80 acres is a distinctly rural horseshoe-shaped ridgetop in the Appalachian foothills.

Julie describes it this way: "Steep slopes fall off on every side of the largely cleared ridgetop. An old commercial orchard once occupied about half of the cleared area; the rest was hayfield. Now it's a songbird ranch, with the orchard all grown up to shrubs and wildflowers, and the hay meadow mown just often enough to keep the sumac in check. Which mostly works.

JULIE ZICKEFOOSE *and her dog, Chet Baker.*

BILL'S PRIMARY *contributions to the habitat improvement involve lots of heavy lifting, such as replanting dead trees as snags near the feeding station.*

"The most dramatic changes have been in species diversity, in both vegetation and birdlife. When we moved in, the hay meadow was being mowed three times each summer, essentially keeping it a huge lawn. The yard was mowed with a brush hog and was choked with Canada thistle. Three plants were in the yard: a forsythia bush, a huge trumpet vine that was running up the south side of the house, and a

THE MEADOW at the Zickefoose–Thompson farm is (predictably) full of nest boxes.

THE VIEW in fall from the birding tower.

POTS WITH bird-friendly blooming plants add color to the understory of a grove of birch trees.

yellow dahlia. We found many box turtle shells in the hay meadow, from animals that had been killed by the zealous mowing regime. We fixed that by mowing much less frequently."

Among the most noticeable and effective improvements we have made is planting gray birch clumps, mulberry trees, a weeping willow, and some big Colorado blue spruces for nesting and roosting. Each of these tree species has made a big difference in attracting birds. The plant species composition of the perennial beds is heavily slanted toward hummingbirds and butterflies, with two beds devoted to cardinal flower (*Lobelia cardinalis*) and two more turned over to tropical and North American salvias. Offering burbling fresh water in a recirculating "Magnificent Bird Spa" has been nothing short of revolutionary, bringing in warblers, vireos, and even bizarre vagrants such as white-winged crossbill and dickcissel!

Julie's favorite feature of our birdy farmyard is its shade gardens—gray birch clumps with container-planted upright fuchsias and geraniums beneath them.

"It's like a little park, and my studio looks right out on it," she says.

"From a human standpoint, the 42-foot-tall bird-watching tower we built atop my studio is the bee's knees. There's nothing like getting well up above your gardens to appreciate the tapestry of color they create, and it's an unparalleled place to fatten one's Big Day list by listening and watching for birds in a 360-degree panoramic view. And I would be remiss if I didn't mention the little greenhouse that gets me through the winter, where I save all the plants I can't live without for next year. I have blossoms year-round, and standing in that humid,

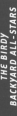

THE BIRDING *tower.*

SUMAC SPECIES *add color to the fall landscape and food for birds and wildlife in the lean winter months.*

hot, sunny space on a frigid winter day fixes me.

"Appalachian Ohio is a pretty lush place; in fact it's spoiled me for wanting to live anywhere else. There's a lovely mix of southern and northern species. Hooded and Kentucky warblers are common in the understory, as are pawpaw trees and spicebush. There is so much natural plant material that feeds birds, so drawing on what's already here gives a very strong foundation to any bird-gardening effort."

The birds' favorite features? "The combination of a small feeding station and the recirculating Magnificent Bird Spa definitely draws the most birds," says Julie. "In spring, you can't beat a newly leafed gray birch for attracting warblers.

A MALE *scarlet tanager bathes in Julie's birdbath.*

Gray birches get chewed on by most every insect pest in the book, so they're natural warbler feeders in spring. By late July, the seed cones have matured, and they start feeding goldfinches and siskins, juncos and tree sparrows well through the winter. Gray birches have it all, and they're beautiful in every season."

We've amassed a flyover/breeder/vagrant yard list of 187 species, with a Kirtland's warbler the most recent visitor, on August 12, 2012. Because we live on a ridgetop, "hill-topping" birds and butterflies migrate along our property, so we've had some truly weird inland records, such as black-crowned night-heron, snow goose, common loon, black-bellied plover, tundra swan, and short-eared owl, as well as both bald

A FAVORITE fall activity is gathering persimmons, a fruit that both birds and humans love.

and golden eagles. Odd passerines include dickcissel, white-winged crossbill, orange-crowned warbler, and several sedge wrens. For whatever reason, we're a fall migration hotspot for Philadelphia vireo—we see about 10 each fall.

The only regret regarding how we've managed this property? From Julie: "We need to buy a bulldozer to battle back the wisteria (an invasive Asian vine species) that is threatening to take over our east hill." From me: I wish we had a pond, but our rocky clay soil and lack of strong natural springs make that mostly a pipe dream.

Advice from Julie, who does most of the gardening on our place: "Bird gardeners need to think of garden plants as each having its own purpose. Ask yourself when shopping, 'Who will like this? How will birds use this plant?' And try to stick to things that birds like. For instance, while highly bred flowers such as fuchsias or impatiens with doubled, ruffled petals look pretty, they offer no entry point for hummingbirds or butterflies, and are often devoid of nectar, anyway. Base your gardens on native plants and you'll have to replace fewer plants. Try to have a succession of bloom, not just in June but through August and September too. Visit your garden centers and other people's gardens in each month of the year to see what's interesting and blooming as the summer wears on. Then sprinkle those plants through your borders so you're never without color.

"Also this: Beware of gift plants; people are often giving them away because they're pulling them out by double handfuls in their own gardens! Watch for plant thugs—there are always plants that will try to turn your garden beds into a monoculture. Impose zero-tolerance on such species, pulling them the minute they emerge. Never walk by a weed without pulling it. If you have a plant that delights you, share it with your friends. That's the greatest joy of gardening."

Connie and Pat Toops

Marshall, North Carolina

USDA ZONE 6

PAT AND *Connie Toops.*

SHORTLY BEFORE PAT TOOPS FINISHED a 30-year National Park Service career in resource management, he and his wife, Connie, found the perfect retirement spot—an old farm in the Appalachian Mountains northwest of Asheville, North Carolina. Since 2002 they've called Lost Cove Farm home, and to their delight, this place often feels as wild as the parks where they formerly lived and worked. Their nearest human neighbor is a mile away; only the moon and stars illuminate the night sky.

Connie writes: "Our 129 acres are flung like a pair of saddlebags over a 3,100-foot mountain ridge. On the east side, steep slopes were logged half a century ago. They are now cloaked in shady hardwood forest dominated by oak, hickory, and tulip poplar trees. Scattered pines crown the western side of that ridge. It descends through overgrown pastures and young hardwood forest to our home, located at elevation 2,500 feet. A gurgling creek tumbles between our house and a north-facing slope covered with mature oaks, hickories, maples, beech trees, and woodland wildflowers. Another forested ridge completes the mountain barrier that encircles Lost Cove. In addition to the log home we built after moving here, the farmstead includes an 1800s log cabin and two log barns. Nearby we have a large vegetable garden, a small orchard, and numerous berry bushes. We normally receive about 45 inches of annual precipitation."

The logging made perfect habitat for golden-winged warblers, which nested on the Toopses' property for six years after their arrival. The old pastures also welcomed indigo buntings, field sparrows, and chestnut-sided warblers. Logged areas were reclaimed by thickets of young trees and brush, perfect for ruffed grouse. The property has countless curves and contours. Pat

THE TOOPSES' *homestead before and after they purchased it.*

135

AN EASTERN *screech-owl nests in a box that Pat Toops built.*

notes that "good wildlife habitat offers lots of diversity and edge effect."

Pat and Connie have made things more attractive to bluebirds, catbirds, brown thrashers, cardinals, and thrushes by planting trees and shrubs such as serviceberry, chokeberry, winterberry, and other native hollies. Traditional seed and suet feeders outside the dining-room window have a backdrop of fruit-bearing trees and bushes, meaning there is always some bird activity to observe.

Connie describes another piece of bird habitat: "We terraced the slope in front of our home and planted a prairie meadow, interspersed with grass strips that allow mowing access and provide walking paths. There's a rainbow of color as prairie natives bloom from late May through August. During summer, song sparrows, goldfinches, and indigo buntings feed in the prairie and nest along its edges. Coneflowers, downy sunflowers, and overarching grasses retain seeds and offer cover in winter. After white-throated sparrows and juncos head north, we burn the prairie to recycle plant nutrients into the soil. When we trim branches and saplings, we construct brush piles that offer refuge from the unexpected swoops of Cooper's, sharp-shinned, and broad-winged hawks.

"One of Pat's hobbies is woodworking, and he's constructed several dozen nest boxes tailored for chickadees, titmice, bluebirds, and screech-owls. Occasionally these boxes have also hosted great crested flycatchers, rough-winged swallows, flying squirrels, and red squirrels. Carolina wrens covet nesting shelves under the front- and back-porch eaves. Eastern phoebes and barn swallows plaster mud nests under porch overhangs. Forty-three percent of the avian species we've observed on our property nest here. We attribute that to quality habitat and thoughtful placement of nesting structures."

The Carolina mountains throw a few challenges at flatlanders (Pat and Connie are originally from Ohio). Steep slopes make it difficult to plant and mow. The Toopses do their best to battle invasive species such as Asian bittersweet, Japanese honeysuckle, Japanese stilt grass, kudzu, and garlic mustard, but complete control is impossible.

One notable disappointment is the loss of golden-winged warblers and a decrease in bobwhite and ruffed grouse that use their property.

These birds thrive in early succession habitats—recently cleared areas with meadows and sparse trees. "The reality of living in our rich, moist climate is that trees grow prolifically. We've tried to cut saplings and brush from fields where golden-wings and quail frolicked, but short of importing goats or cattle, we can't keep pace with the encroaching forest. Edges and thickets are becoming overgrown with trees that thrive in the southern Appalachians. So we now savor morning songs of scarlet tanagers and evening calls of barred owls that come with these forest changes," Connie explains.

BARN SWALLOWS *nest on several of the Toopses' buildings.*

Connie continues: "Pat and I have shared many incredible birding moments at Lost Cove. It's hard to decide whether a drumming ruffed grouse trumps an autumn afternoon when a peregrine falcon circled us as we sat in amazement on our mountaintop. Or another afternoon when at that same spot, some 350 broad-winged hawks soared south in migration. Yet we agree our most remarkable avian visitor was the lone whip-poor-will that spent an April night in a tree near our bedroom window.

THE TOOPSES' *Lost Cove Farm is a mixture of woods, meadows, and edge habitat.*

We loved hearing these mournful night-singers in other places where we've lived, but whip-poor-wills were never common here, and their numbers are seriously declining. To have one all to ourselves, lulling us to sleep, was an occasion that may never be repeated here. The memory carved a special place in our hearts."

The Toopses have just a single regret about the way their birdy property has turned out: they didn't think to put in a small pond while the bulldozer was there as they built their home. This feature still remains on their "wish" list for future habitat enhancements.

Connie has this last bit of advice: "One year we mounted a nest box under the gable of our log home, and we were thrilled when it attracted nesting rough-winged swallows. Unknown to us, the box became infested with brown chicken mites from feathers that the adult swallows gathered at a local barnyard to line the nest. After the babies fledged, hungry mites roamed into our bedroom, where they made themselves at home in our clothing, bed, and feather pillows. Getting rid of those pesky mites was a nightmare! So our advice for improving your backyard for birds is this: Keep birds in your yard. Never mount a nest box on your home!"

Andy Kinsey

Gainesville, Georgia

USDA ZONE 7

ANDY KINSEY.

ANDY ADDED this pond to his property shortly after moving in.

ANDY KINSEY AND HIS WIFE, JENNIFER, and their three young children live about an hour north of Atlanta in Gainesville, Georgia. Andy moved to Georgia when he was nine years old and was raised on a farm about 10 miles from his current residence. He works that farm with his oldest brother, selling pumpkins in the fall and then Christmas trees, and growing ornamental trees and shrubs year-round for landscape use.

Andy describes how his interest in birds and farming coexist: "As I have been an avid birder for the last 20 years, the farm actually works quite nicely into my birding 'needs.' We grow several species of trees and shrubs that produce berries that are highly attractive to birds and oodles of different evergreens that can be added to any landscape to increase wintering habitat. Ultimately, it means that the farm is loaded with great birds throughout the year, but also that I can plant many of those same trees and shrubs in my yard at home too! It's a pretty sweet deal and I highly recommend it as a job for birders!"

He continues: "About 10 years ago, when I realized I would likely be living in north Georgia for quite some time, my wife and I began searching for property that would suit our needs. We ended up finding a small subdivision about 50 miles north of Atlanta. The subdivision was designed with an 'environment first' strategy in which a heavily forested tract was divided into 1- and 2-acre lots. We toured through the subdivision and discovered that several of the lots backed up to a 15-acre forested wetland with an active beaver population. We chose a site with natural springs flanking the property and a large open beaver pond immediately behind what would become our home."

PURPLE MARTINS *nest in the martin houses near the pond.*

Most of the property was forested by a mature stand of hardwoods, including white and red oaks, hickory, tulip poplar, sourwood, and beech trees, all easily reaching 60 feet in height. Given that the canopy was so mature, there wasn't much of an understory, but what was there consisted of several species of wildlife-friendly trees, including dogwood, serviceberry, and red buckeye.

Having forested natural springs on both sides of the property and a large wooded wetland behind them gave the Kinseys a nice start, but there were still several enhancements that they wanted to make. As they built their home, they had a small, shallow pond (about 2 feet deep) added in the backyard. The initial intent was for it to be used as a breeding pool for several species of woodland salamanders and the 10 or so species of frogs and toads inhabiting the property. In addition to this pond, several years later the Kinseys cooperated with their neighbors to add a larger and much deeper pond (about 9 feet deep) on the other side of the yard.

THE SEEPING *spring that feeds the Kinseys' pond is a naturally birdy spot.*

They also made some improvements to the property's flora, through both addition and subtraction. They selectively removed some of the smaller and weaker sweet gum, red maple, and tulip trees and began adding some of what Andy calls the "wildlife-attracting tree champions."

"There are several must-have plants for all yards in our zone (Zone 7), and while I don't have all of them in our yard yet, I do fully intend to plant them! We have added several tree species that produce berries and nuts: 'Wildfire' black gum, 'Autumn Brilliance' serviceberry, Allegheny chinkapin, common pawpaw, and we're also blessed to have huge tulip poplar (quite attractive to orioles when in flower), hickory, and more than our fair share of beech trees (which produce

WOOD DUCK boxes.

hordes of nuts during the fall and are wildly popular with a multitude of animals). We were still missing one of the greatest deciduous trees of all: the bald cypress. So we began creating a fairly substantial grove of bald cypress (we now have 18 scattered throughout our yard in and around all of the wetland areas). Bald cypress is the South's most magnificent contribution to the large tree flora and can actually be planted in up to a foot of water with no associated problems. It is not only elegant and stately, but it's also a member of a very small group of deciduous conifers that are insanely attractive to insects and therefore to foraging migrant warblers. This is a must-have tree for all yards that can handle their magnitude and that have the right growing conditions!" (As a side note, Andy adds that there is a newer form of bald cypress known as 'Falling Waters' that has an upright central leader with strongly weeping secondary branching, thus making this incredible tree more space-appropriate for yards with confined boundaries.)

The Kinseys then began to add evergreen trees to their property. These provide nesting habitat for birds during summer, cover during the winter months, and places to forage throughout migration. They have focused on two main evergreens: the native eastern hemlock (which is now suffering a decline from the hemlock woolly adelgid) and the non-native and noninvasive Japanese cedar (*Cryptomeria ja-*

ponica). Both attain heights beyond 40 feet in Zone 7 and provide terrific habitat for nesting birds, foraging migrant warblers, nuthatches, creepers, woodpeckers, and roosting owls.

"We have also added a few deodar cedars and several small blue atlas cedars," reports Andy. "These are not only beautiful trees but will also help us achieve diversity in our large evergreen habitat. When space permits, I plan to add some of the newer red leaf hollies (they are thick evergreens with loads of berries for the birds)."

In more recent years, their plant diversifying efforts have focused on smaller shrubs for food and cover. Examples include rabbiteye blueberries, 'Celeste' figs, dwarf 'Hiromi' cherries, 'Brilliantissima' chokeberry, the irresistible 'Pink Lemonade' hybrid blueberry, mountain laurel, Abelia, and wax myrtle. Wintering sparrows and kinglets find the wax myrtle's density appealing, and early spring–arriving warblers regularly use them for foraging too.

Says Andy, "With a moderate amount of work over the past seven years, my wife and I have been able to transform our yard from a mediocre landscape for attracting birds and other wildlife into a real birding and wildlife haven.

"To date we have seen 124 species of birds in our yard, with a whopping 25 species of warblers, including nesting hooded warblers and Louisiana waterthrush in our swales, and loads of migrant warblers, including blackpoll, bay-breasted, prothonotary, Cape May, Blackburnian, and cerulean. The two small ponds we added and the large beaver pond behind us have rewarded us with numerous ducks, herons (including American bittern in most years), foraging flycatchers, and a belted king-

ANDY HAS let a portion of his property grow up into brushy field habitat.

fisher! We have even managed to attract unlikely visitors such as an adult bald eagle and a small community of red-headed woodpeckers.

"Our little enhancements to our property have provided us with years of delight and enjoyment. I hope that I can pass these treasures down to my children and grandchildren."

Terry and Marci Fuller

San Benito, Texas

USDA ZONE 9A

TERRY AND Marci Fuller.

IN THE 16 YEARS since Terry and Marci Fuller bought their sprawling ranch house on a bit more than an acre in the Rio Grande Valley of south Texas, their habitat improvements have been so transformative that the list of birds and other species attracted to it would make a person wide-eyed with disbelief. Three of the current 20 U.S. records for green-breasted mango, a Neotropical hummingbird, have been recorded in their yard.

Marci describes the start of this transformation: "When we moved in, our house had the standard-issue suburban lawn with a few scattered trees. Oh yes, and some beds of flowers. Plastic flowers. We spent the first months pulling plastic out of the yard. The biggest asset was the frontage along a *resaca,* an oxbow lake formed by an old channel of the Rio Grande. Having this body of water nearby was going to make our job a lot easier, because we knew it would attract lots of birds and wildlife."

Their property is classified as subtropical riparian habitat, so the Fullers did a lot of research as they made their plans to improve and restore it. "We supported our local native plant growers, but most of the plants were rescues from other sites, like native habitat that was being bulldozed for development. We'd even rescue and transplant

STREET VIEWS of the Fullers' property, from when they moved in and from more recently.

THE FULLERS' front yard as it was.

THE FRONT yard as it is now.

tiny seedlings coming up in sidewalk cracks. What's a weed to most peoples' eyes was never a weed to Terry," Marci added.

They began restoring the property using native plants that would thrive in a riparian habitat. Where once there was a rectangle of mowed grass, within a few years there were dense thickets with trails winding from the house to the resaca and back. These thickets and the other subtropical plant growth in the yard soon became home to a family of plain chachalacas, a large, chickenlike bird that is resident in south Texas, plus many of the other avian specialties of that region.

There were some hard decisions, realizations, and compromises along the way—like letting the butterfly caterpillars eat all the leaves of a rare native tree and accepting the mosquitoes that come with the deep foliage. But overall the Fullers are thrilled with the transformation. And from the looks of their list of backyard visitors, all the hard work is paying off!

"Our yard is now famous for its lists—birds, butterflies, odonates (dragonflies)—and also its rarity records. We had the fifth U.S. record for green-breasted mango hummingbird, plus really special bird species such as mangrove

BEFORE AND after views of the central path in the Fullers' backyard.

BEFORE AND after views of the walkway to the resaca behind the Fullers' home.

cuckoo, crimson-collared grosbeak, and dusky-capped flycatcher. Our special butterfly species include sightings of erato heliconia and Blomfield's beauty. And as Terry has mastered dragonfly identifica-

THE FULLERS' property has earned a designation as wildlife-friendly habitat from the state of Texas.

tion, he's found a lot of exciting and rare species in our yard. We have multiple U.S. records—claret pondhawk, black pondhawk, evening skimmer, and pale-green darners."

Favorite plants in the Fullers' restored habitat include Barbados cherry, potato trees, and mistflower— all good food sources for birds and bugs alike.

Marci adds: "We've also planted a grove of sabal palms, complete with an understory of native passion flower and rare David's milkberry. These palms used to line the Rio Grande centuries ago, but only scarce remnants remain owing to habitat loss from agriculture and development."

Two bits of advice the Fullers have for their fellow bird gardeners in the South: If you have nearby neighbors, make sure your property border plants are people-friendly (nothing thorny or invasive). And be prepared to tolerate the critters that come along with the native vegetation and habitat that you are restoring.

Marci: "It's remarkable how even a little restored patch of native habitat such as our property is rediscovered by the creatures that live here, and how important it becomes."

Dudley Edmondson

Duluth, Minnesota

USDA ZONE 4

LIKE MANY OF OUR other birdy backyard all-stars, Dudley Edmondson faced some challenges when he purchased his suburban property in Duluth, Minnesota. The first challenge: it was already landscaped, but with plants, shrubs, and trees that were for visual appeal to humans, not for the benefit of birds and wildlife. He needed to replace the landscape left by the previous owners with more bird-friendly habitat and features, and he began to do that shortly after moving in. And this was when he encountered the second challenge: the quality of the soil in his new backyard. It was full of junk from decades of trash dumping and burning. It took several years of attempting to clean up the soil and replace it with better medium before

NANCY AND Dudley Edmondson.

Dudley and his wife, Nancy, hit on the idea of using raised beds for the wildlife-friendly gardens (Dudley's area of endeavor) and the herb and vegetable gardens (Nancy's domain).

The Edmondsons' property is a modest-sized, rectangular suburban plot with the house and a few small gardens in the front half and the bird and wildlife gardens in the back half. Over the past two decades, Dudley has enhanced the property with native and bird-

THE BACKYARD bed before Dudley's improvements.

THE BACKYARD bed after improvements.

145

THE ENTRANCE to the Edmondsons' backyard.

THE DECK near the backyard pond is the Edmondsons' favorite spot.

friendly species, with a special focus on fruit-bearing trees and shrubs, including highbush cranberry, juneberry, chokecherry, and elderberry, in addition to encouraging the mountain ash, paper birch, and maple trees that were already present on the property.

Adding water seemed important since there is no naturally occurring source nearby. "There was a depression in the backyard that was full of bits of junk from years of trash burning by prior residents. I cleaned out a lot of it, filled in the depression, and then mounded up new soil around the area to create a pond. It's got a rubber liner and a recirculating pump, so it functions just like a mini wetland. I planted water lilies, water hyacinth, and several sedges in pots and placed them in the pond. I also planted the mounded edges with flowering plants such as thyme, sedums, more irises, and arrowhead, which really added to the natural look of the water feature," Dudley said.

A deck that is built out to the edge of the pond is a favorite sitting spot for Dudley and Nancy at dinnertime. "It's amazing to sit there and see what comes in to the water. It's not just birds, but butterflies, dragonflies and damselflies, and aquatic insects, such as water beetles and water striders. Our wireless connection also reaches out there so I can sit and watch and pretend to be working! The pond is definitely our favorite feature of our property," said Dudley.

Nice as they are for the birds and wildlife, these enhancements serve another purpose. As a fulltime professional wildlife photographer and videographer, Dudley knew these enhancements would bring in birds and other creatures for him to photograph. "I've gotten a lot of excellent images right here at home!"

THE BIRDY
BACKYARD ALL-STARS

A small greenhouse gives the Edmondsons a head start on the summer growing season. One raised-bed garden specifically aimed at butterflies is filled with plants such as common milkweed, butterfly weed, liatris (or blazing star), black-eyed Susan, purple coneflower, and royal catchfly. A stand of tall woodland sunflower is the main focal point for the local American goldfinches, which use its fibers for nest building in late summer and eat its seed in the autumn.

At the feeding stations, the black-capped chickadees, red- and white-breasted nuthatches, and various finches enjoy black-oil sunflower and Nyjer seed. Nest boxes have hosted families of house wrens and chickadees. But the primary bird-attracting features are the fruit-bearing trees and shrubs, which lure in flocks of American robins, cedar and Bohemian waxwings, and red- and white-winged crossbills. All this bird activity also brings in other birds, including a rare in-town appearance of boreal chickadee, boreal and great gray owls, and two rare vagrants from the West: Townsend's solitaire and varied thrush.

Dudley still sees some room for improvement. "I'm trying to create more nesting habitat for birds—shrubby and brushy areas where cardinals and sparrows can nest and where others can roost. And you can't have too many fruit-producing plants, so I'm sure we'll plant more of those," he said.

It seems a birdy backyard all-star's work is never done.

A CLOSER look at the backyard pond.

DUDLEY ADDED a few birdhouses to the backyard plan.

Steve and Cheryl Eno

Raymond, Nebraska

USDA ZONE 5B

STEVE AND *Cheryl Eno.*

NEST BOXES *line the path through the meadow at the home of Steve and Cheryl Eno.*

BEFORE STEVE AND CHERYL ENO built their dream house on 10 rural acres near Raymond, Nebraska, they spent a decade visiting the land, having picnics, hiking around, and talking about their plans for the land. Steve, a mason, built the house himself, out of brick. It sits on a rise, just above two ponds, which the Enos had dug out and enlarged soon after they moved into the house. They immediately set about improving the habitat for birds and wildlife.

"The place had a decent number of trees for this part of Nebraska, which is mostly wide open. We did a lot of additional planting for wildlife, bought 10 additional acres adjoining our land, and set aside a several-acre patch that we keep in native grasses," Steve explained.

In addition to the habitat improvements, Steve and Cheryl also established and maintain three large feeding stations and a total of 14 feeders. This sounds like a lot of feeders even before you learn that the Enos feed about 2,000 pounds of cracked corn and other foods per month during the winter. The feeders attract a lot of birds, including flocks of wild turkey, coveys of northern bobwhite, and a variety of sparrows, including Harris's sparrow. They also attract quite a few deer, which enjoy sheltering in the grove of pines uphill from the feeders.

Bluebirds have always been a passion for the Enos — Steve and Cheryl are longtime members of the North American Bluebird Society and the founders of Bluebirds Across Nebraska (BAN). The large barn adjacent to their house includes a woodworking shop where Steve and his friends have built thousands of nest boxes for BAN. Steve has become an expert at determining whether a nest box is built with the proper materials, dimensions, and entrance size. One look in his basement reveals dozens upon dozens of nest boxes and nest-box prototypes sent in by everyone from individual bluebird landlords to commercial manufacturers seeking Steve's input and endorsement.

Yet it's outside the Enos' house and barn that nest boxes have been put to their highest and intended use. Numerous pairs of eastern bluebirds and tree swallows nest in boxes on the Enos' property. Every year eastern screech-owls have used one or more of the larger nest boxes Steve and Cheryl have put up, intended for northern flickers. The wood duck boxes and mallard nesting platforms on the ponds get regular use. A 55-gallon drum cut open and laid on its side and pole-mounted in one of the ponds was another nest box the Enos provided, hoping to attract Canada geese. The most recent tenants to use the drum were rather unusual—a pair of great horned owls, which successfully raised two owlets.

THE WETLAND habitat on the Enos' property attracts a lot of birds and insects.

THE VIEW down to the pond from the Enos' house.

The past two years have seen a return of a former nesting species on the Enos' property: black-capped chickadees.

"We used to have chickadees nesting in our boxes and visiting our feeders, but West Nile virus really decimated their population around here in 2002. It took 10 years, but this spring we finally have chickadees in our nest boxes again," Steve explained.

A VARIETY of birds have used the Enos' nest boxes near the ponds.

While the birds and wildlife throng to the Enos' feeding stations, Steve and Cheryl's favorite feature of their place is the paths around the ponds.

"We love walking the paths with our dogs. You never know what you're going to see. One year we had an osprey on the ponds, which was special," Steve said.

"I love watching the feeders we can see from our kitchen windows," Cheryl adds. "In winter we get larger numbers of turkeys and bob-white, and in summer the Baltimore orioles come in for a bit of grape jelly we put out. It's just such a peaceful way to begin and end the day, watching the birds come and go."

Lynn Hassler

Tucson, Arizona

USDA ZONE 9A

WHEN LYNN HASSLER MOVED into her suburban Tucson home 26 years ago, the small, pie-shaped lot had limited ground space and a lot of brick patio. The yard had attractive but sparse plantings in the patio area and a hot tub that took up way too much space. However, the back wall bordered a hillside corridor of natural Sonoran Desert vegetation, which vastly increased the appeal of the property.

LYNN HASSLER.

Her first improvement might seem odd to the average homeowner, but perfectly sensible to the bird gardener: she removed the hot tub and some of the brick patio to make room for more plants.

Lynn describes the transformation of the habitat like this: "By planting all available ground space, I significantly increased the amount of cover and shelter for birds and wildlife. I added many container plants to further transform the empty patio into a relatively lush garden. Two simple water features—planter bottoms that I hand clean and fill—have made a huge difference in my yard's attractiveness. One water feature is above my back wall in the desert and is visited by many birds as well as javelina, bobcat, cottontail, coyote, and the occasional ring-tailed cat and gray fox. The other water dish sits in the patio where many of my yard birds come to enjoy a drink or to bathe."

A GARDEN wall marks the boundary between Lynn Hassler's backyard and the desert beyond.

Her favorite feature in her birdy backyard is actually the surrounding desert. "Since my planted garden is relatively small, I have time to give those plants plenty of TLC, but my yard truly benefits from the juxtaposition of nearby native desert vegetation: brittlebush, saguaro, cholla, barrel, and prickly pear cactus, creosote, ocotillo, palo verde, mesquite, and sweet acacia all grow in the desert habitat beyond my back wall. Birds such as pyrrhuloxia, western screech-owl, phainopepla, and brown-crested flycatcher rarely come down into my patio garden but are evident on the adjacent desert hillside. I like to think of my gardening as a slightly more lush extension of that habitat."

Very high temperatures for six months of the year, plus extreme aridity, necessitate using native or low-water-use plants for the bird gardener in the southwestern desert region. Adding to the challenge is the fact that it freezes in Lynn's region nearly every winter—occasionally for prolonged periods.

Lynn describes her favorite backyard plant: "My favorite addition

ONE OF Lynn's favorite plants is the Baja fairy duster.

THE PATIO is surrounded by bird-friendly plants.

is the prized Baja fairy duster (*Calliandra californica*), a medium-sized shrub that sports scarlet puff-ball blooms. The flowers are an orgy of pollination, attracting hummingbirds galore, verdins, butterflies, and all manner of iridescent bees and flies that I can't even begin to identify. An added bonus is that it's a host plant for the caterpillars of several blue butterflies. Cactus wrens and other bug eaters stop by to devour the caterpillars and insects, and although it's only about 5 feet tall, its dense habit makes for good cover and shelter. A close second is the humongous non-native pyracantha (15 feet by 15 feet) that grows in my front yard. In winter this plant draws in higher-elevation birds that descend into the lowlands for food, including American robin, hermit thrush, western bluebird, and cedar waxwing. The local birds relish the berries as well."

Lynn lists violet-crowned hummingbird, rose-breasted grosbeak, Townsend's solitaire, rufous-backed robin, and yellow-breasted chat among the more unusual species to visit her yard.

Asked if she'd like a do-over on any of her bird-gardening decisions, she said: "I would've planted a native tree in the space where the hot tub was removed instead of shorter-growing shrubs and perennials. It wasn't feasible at the time because of another large tree (non-native Chinese elm), which eventually crashed down on my house in a monsoon-generated microburst. Other than that, I'm happy with the changes and additions I've made."

Her property has produced a yard list of 124 species to date, along with some epic bird events. "In August of 1993 I had a seven-hummingbird-species day: Calliope, Anna's, black-chinned, Costa's, rufous, broad-tailed, and broad-billed hummingbirds. An elf owl that spent several days roosting in my elm tree was a treat."

She enjoys the gangs of Gambel's quail that visit the yard every day of the year. And she gets many migrant birds thanks to her proximity to Sabino Canyon, a desert riparian habitat a 1/2 mile away at the base of the Santa Catalina Mountain range. Her garden is a good stopover for birds headed up the mountain (the summit of Mt. Lemmon is 9,157 feet).

"Because I live in an area of great hummingbird and butterfly diversity, that's primarily what I think about in terms of new plantings, though I've essentially used up my ground space. More containers are possible, but the summer watering is quite a chore. I might work my way up into the desert, perhaps enhancing my space with some indigenous wildflowers."

Kathy Wiederholt

Carrington, North Dakota

USDA ZONE 4

LIKE MANY HOUSES IN NORTH DAKOTA, Kathy Wiederholt's was moved into town. It was built on a farm near Sykeston, North Dakota, more than 100 years ago. When the original owner decided to move into the small town of Carrington, she brought along the house and a grainery that was turned into a garage. Kathy and her husband bought the property in 2004 and have been making small improvements ever since.

KATHY WIEDERHOLT.

Kathy describes the property and location: "We have a double, corner lot on the southwest side of town. We really like the location because we are only a few blocks from 'the country' and a 20-minute drive from the Coteau, the rolling hills of grassland dotted with prairie 'potholes'—small bodies of water that were left behind by retreating glaciers."

Nearby hayfields and undeveloped areas make this the quiet part of town, which is good for residents both human and avian. Like much of the Great Plains, the area around Carrington is mostly wide-open agricultural fields and grasslands. In towns and around rural

THE WIEDERHOLTS' *backyard before any improvements and the more bird-friendly backyard today.*

homesteads, clusters of trees and shrubs are planted to serve as windbreaks— structures against the howling winter winds and shelter for creatures.

"Wide open" also describes the property when the Wiederholts purchased it. Most of it was lawn or stone mulch, catering to the previous owners' low-maintenance preferences. A cluster of trees—mostly box elder—along the northwest corner of the property formed the beginning of some sheltering habitat. To this Kathy added a variety of drought- and cold-tolerant shrubs, creating a perfect out-of-the-wind spot for the bird feeders. To Kathy's regular year-round feeder offerings of Nyjer and black-oil sunflower seed, she adds venison suet in winter to give the birds some extra energy in the harsh North Dakota weather. Birds use this corner in all seasons for foraging and roosting, and for nesting in summer. Spruce and ash trees and a chokecherry thicket in the next-door neighbor's yard further enhance the bird-friendliness of the immediate area. Shelterbelts of habitat such as this also serve to hold snow on the ground, helping keep both soil and moisture in place until the spring thaw.

VIEWS OF *the Wiederholts' front yard, before and after habitat improvements.*

The Wiederholts' favorite parts of the property are the gardens near the kitchen and driveway. They've placed feeders here so they can view the feeding action from both the kitchen and the living room. Kathy leaves the dormant plants standing in winter for foraging chickadees, nuthatches, finches, and sparrows. She adds a birdbath to these gardens in summer, and it gets a lot of takers during the long, hot dry spells in July and August.

Among the challenges Kathy has faced as a North Dakota bird gardener is the difficulty in growing trees. She describes it this way:

A VARIETY of layers in the yard cater to the changing needs of birds.

"It's hard to grow trees here as almost all the trees you dream about aren't native to North Dakota, nor are they hardy. It's quite dry here, with only about 18 to 19 inches of moisture annually. And it's often extremely windy with huge temperature swings: it can be really cold and then very warm within a few days. It's tough on trees. We try to make the environment friendlier by mulching under all of our trees, shrubs, and plants. However, in July and August we still have to water our trees if the weather is dry, to avoid losing them. This is a huge change for me, having lived in a heavily forested part of Wisconsin."

The Wiederholts' efforts to keep their trees alive are paying off for the birds. The large spruce tree in the corner of their lot serves as bird central in the winter when coveys of gray partridge fly in from the fields to the south. They forage beneath the spruce and then cozy up under the low-hanging branches to roost for the night. Other birds use the spruce for shelter too, including purple finches, goldfinches, common redpolls, and pine siskins.

Occasionally a rare and unusual bird finds its way to the Wiederholts' backyard. One winter their feeders hosted a single male hoary redpoll among a flock of common redpolls. And in 2008 Kathy witnessed another exciting influx of birds. "For about a week in early May, we were inundated with sparrows: white-crowned, white-throated, song, fox, and Harris's sparrows, plus a single spotted towhee. Late-spring blizzards drove these birds to search for any available food or shelter, and our yard was one of the places where they found it. Every day they would forage in the garden beds, often scratching with their feet, flinging the wood chips 4 feet out into the driveway. Every evening I would sweep the chips back into the flower beds and scatter more seed for the birds!"

The bluebird houses they have mounted on opposite sides of the yard have yet to attract their intended tenants, but house wrens nest in them every year. Kathy describes the scene: "We love to watch the adult wrens feeding the chicks. Every few minutes they fly up and land on our fence near the box with an insect in their bill. They sit casually, looking around to see if the coast is clear before entering the nest box. We've never seen the fledglings leave the nest or in the yard—they're just gone."

Common visitors to the Wiederholts' yard include American robin, mourning dove, chipping sparrow, Brewer's blackbird, purple and house finches, American goldfinch, western kingbird, house wren, black-capped chickadee, white-breasted nuthatch, and pine siskin, with the occasional passing visit by sharp-shinned and Cooper's hawks. Among the exciting migrants that have stopped by are mourning warbler, tree sparrow, rose-breasted grosbeak, hermit thrush, white-winged crossbill, Baltimore oriole, and American redstart.

Kathy sums up her birdy backyard efforts like this: "We don't try to keep our plants and gardens too tidy—our birds seem to like the brushy, messy parts best. We keep our grass long in summer (3 inches or taller) to conserve water. We rarely use pesticides, and we don't try to eliminate every single weed. This guarantees that there will be more insects, caterpillars, grubs, weed seeds—basically more diversity—and the birds need all this and more."

John and Durrae Johanek

West Bozeman, Montana

USDA ZONE 4

JOHN AND DURRAE JOHANEK came to West Bozeman, Montana, from Pennsylvania in 1992 seeking a new home—one that had some elbow room (no close neighbors) and a view of the surrounding mountain ranges. They found it in the foothills of the Bridger Mountains, just outside this thriving western town. Their property consists of 5 acres, 4 of which are open grassland. It lies at an elevation of approximately 1 mile, which is about 500 feet higher than nearby Bozeman.

When the Johaneks moved in, the entire property was wide open, save for a few saplings the previous owner had planted in order to make it look more appealing to a buyer. John and Durrae immediately set about adding some variety to their habitat, planting many trees and shrubs—evergreen as well as deciduous. To get immediate results, they brought in large mature evergreens, and they've added one or two each year since. They also installed two "pond" water features, many bird feeders, and birdhouses to increase the attractiveness of the new habitat. They established brush piles in the large meadow, which have given shelter to birds and small mammals alike.

"Our favorite features are the pond water features. They provide water and bathing for not only our birds but also resident deer,

JOHN AND *Durrae Johanek.*

THE JOHANEKS' *property when they first moved in.*

TODAY'S MORE *bird-friendly version.*

157

THE BACKYARD patio pond has been a big hit with the local birds and wildlife.

PLENTY OF weather–blocking shelter benefits the birds in harsh winter weather.

skunks, rabbits, raccoons, and the occasional snake and toad. Plus, the trickling sound is soothing," Durrae explains. In winter they shut down the ponds, but they leave one small birdbath out and operational with a heating unit.

Bird gardening in this growing zone is not a walk in the park. The main challenges to healthy vegetation are the climate, soil, and deer. The soil is clay, the climate is dry, and the growing season is very short.

"We plant only native plant species, but even they struggle. What does grow, the deer either eat into submission or rub their antlers on, often killing the plant. As a result, we have to fence nearly everything," Durrae explains.

One bad side effect of the Johaneks' efforts at creating sheltering habitat has been the appearance of house sparrows on the property.

"When we moved here, there were no house sparrows anywhere near us. And we were thrilled when we got mountain bluebirds nesting in the half-dozen boxes we put up for them. In a couple of years, the house sparrows moved in, and despite all efforts to get rid of them, they took over the bluebird houses, to the point that we had to take all of them down. We now have houses only for wrens and chickadees." (The small entrance holes that these tiny birds can use exclude the chunkier house sparrows from gaining entry.)

Backyard birding highlights are many for the Johaneks. One year they had, in addition to the resident great-horned owls, a northern pygmy-owl and a northern saw-whet owl, only a month apart. The pygmy-owl sat on their deck railing, where it was joined by another. The two birds flew off, and John and Durrae could hear them calling in the nearby foothills. Other interesting visitors and flyovers have included red and white-winged crossbills, sandhill crane, pinyon and Steller's jays, rufous hummingbird, and Bohemian waxwing.

The Johaneks have no regrets about the bird-gardening decisions they have made. "The mature trees we brought in were expensive, so each year we put in what our budget would allow. But we really feel they were well worth it. As the first big conifer (about 25 feet tall) was being lowered into its hole by the tree spade, a robin landed on the top, and we decided we had made a good purchase!

A LOCAL black-billed magpie is fascinated with a decorative concrete raven.

"The brush piles have positive and negative aspects: they have become a real hangout for the house sparrows, but we often see a goshawk or sharp-shinned hawk perched on top of them, looking for and usually enjoying a sparrow dinner."

They hang out hummingbird feeders in early May but have to include a temporary roof to keep off the inevitable spring snows. And they face other bird-feeding challenges: to keep magpies off the suet cakes, they use a double-caged and rather unattractive feeder set-up, but it works. However, even their best efforts have not deterred the black bears that visit in fall. The bears have made short work of the shepherd's crook hanger, bending it down like it was a paper clip. One bold bruin feasted for an hour on the suet dough as the Johaneks watched from inside the house.

SOME OF the local wildlife is almost too friendly.

"We weren't certain what to expect when we moved here, but one morning in our first spring we looked out the kitchen window and saw an adult bald eagle sitting on a fencepost along our driveway. A pair of golden eagles was soaring overhead (we later learned that they nest in the hills behind us)—we were pretty sure we had made a good move," John concluded.

Alvaro Jaramillo

Half Moon Bay, California

USDA ZONES 9-10

ALVARO JARAMILLO.

THE JARAMILLO FAMILY lives in the coastal town of Half Moon Bay, California, which has a population of about 12,000 people. Alvaro works at home much of the time, writing about birds and doing planning and logistics for the many birding tours he leads each year. As is typical in coastal California, the Jaramillos' suburban property is fairly small—the full lot is 60 feet by 120 feet, and half of that is taken up by the house. But Half Moon Bay is surrounded by rural and natural open space, so while their property is modest in size, the proximity of good habitat and the ocean adds greatly to the "birdiness" of the setting.

Alvaro describes the climate as being between growing zones: "The USDA growing zone here is at the changeover from 9 to 10, but here the growing zone nomenclature has its limitations. Since it is based on average temperatures, we come out pretty high, but we have very little variation in temperature from summer to winter, and it never gets hot here! So you can plant Washingtonia palms, which hooded orioles love, but you can't grow a tomato and have it ripen. We don't get enough heat or sun. Instead, we feel the influence of cold ocean winds, particularly in the middle of summer."

Their house was new when they moved in, but the landscaping was a mere afterthought. There were a few garden plants that had been plopped into the ground out front, but no landscaping at all in the backyard. There were a few old dying cottonwood trees that were getting wind burned.

"It was a pretty lame backyard," Alvaro says.

He continues: "I have tried to think carefully about water use, and have put in plants that do not need watering. We have a small lawn patch in the back for the dogs and kids to play on, but we are thinking of getting rid of that in a few years too. I planted native and drought-tolerant plants along the edges of the yard and at the fence line with an emphasis on hummingbirds and a little thicket for the wintering golden-crowned and white-crowned sparrows."

His favorite part of the property is the corner that he can see from his home office window. It has a lot of shrubby cover and a short California wax myrtle tree that attracts a lot of insects. It tends to be where the avian oddities show up, like a clay-colored sparrow one November and a spotted towhee in May. This is also where Alvaro has strategically placed his feeding station, which the birds began using immediately.

"In my region the concerns for any gardener are water use—at least if you are trying to be responsible with resources—and the ocean influence. The latter you just have to deal with. In our front yard we get strong, constant wind and ample salt spray in winter and on windy spring days. Many plants just wither and die, and there is nothing you can do about it. The key is to find plants that will survive in that climate, and often that means California native plants, particularly those from islands or coasts.

"There has been a lot of trial and error trying to figure out what will survive here, so perhaps I had to go through all of that to know what works, but it was frustrating, to say the least. I do think I now understand the importance of having some good shrubbery as cover. Shrubs, and not tall trees, are what survive best here. It took me a while to figure that out."

Living on the California coast, the Jaramillos are smack in the middle of a fall migration path, which means any vagrant birds are likely to bump into the coast, and head for the first patch of sheltering or foraging habitat they find.

ALVARO JARAMILLO'S *backyard is small but very bird-friendly.*

Alvaro relishes these sightings: "I have seen many lost species thousands of miles from where they should be, like prothonotary, prairie, Virginia's, Lucy's, blackpoll, and chestnut-sided warblers—just to mention a few. A white-winged dove, normally a desert resident, was neat to see here too. From the end of my driveway I have a pretty good view of the ocean, so being able to see sooty shearwaters, migrating loons and brant, along with red phalarope,

ORANGE-CROWNED WARBLER.

common murre, and the odd migrating gray whale adds a touch of spice! I know these aren't birds that are attracted by my bird-gardening efforts, but it's really cool to have them on my yard list."

He continues: "Yard birding is one of the most rewarding aspects of birding because it means having to always pay attention. Whenever I am home, I can be birding. This is important to me because with little kids, work deadlines, and trying to run my business from home, I do not have much time to go birding afield! My recreational birding is largely in my yard or around the neighborhood when I walk my dog. Rather than feeling limited by my constraints, I feel really happy to have a spot where the birding can be exciting and unpredictable. I look forward to my next new yard bird or when something new occurs in the local bird community. Watching new birds arrive as your plants grow and your backyard habitat evolves and improves is fantastic to see."

WHITE-CROWNED SPARROW.

John Riutta

Scappoose, Oregon

USDA ZONE 8A

IN 2003, backyard all-star John Riutta and his family bought a suburban home on the outskirts of Scappoose, Oregon. As a bird watcher and naturalist, John could see the potential in the property, and even more bird-friendly habitat in the immediate surroundings.

John describes the setting of his property this way: "We're in a small development on the hill overlooking the town of Scappoose and 'Scappoose Bottom,' an area of reclaimed river bottomland now kept dry by a human-made dike and used primarily for the raising of decorative nursery plants and open-pit gravel mining. The hillside is still rather heavily forested, dominant tree species being Douglas-fir, western hemlock, big leaf maple, red alder, and black cottonwood. Sections of this have been cleared for cul-de-sac housing developments for commuters from Portland—the state's major urban area located approximately 25 miles to the southeast. Our property backs to a small ravine still thickly wooded with Douglas-fir trees. This ravine forms a minor flyway for local migrant birds as well as a number of mammal species. At the bottom of the ravine runs a small seasonal stream."

The property's previous owners were dedicated to having their home featured in lifestyle magazines and had landscaped the area in a style that is unique to the Pacific Northwest, employing more than a dozen different Japanese maples along with an assortment of other non-native species. This was beautiful to look at but did not hold much in the way of foraging or sheltering opportunities for birds and wildlife.

John rid the property of most of the non-native plants left by the former owners and tried to plant more native species. He also has left

JOHN RIUTTA.

THE WOODED ravine behind the Riuttas' home.

THE BACK *terrace offers a peaceful spot for relaxing and bird watching.*

FEEDERS THAT *John added make the yard even more attractive to birds.*

LUSH HABITAT *along a shaded path on the Riuttas' property.*

the ravine entirely undeveloped, including fallen trees that are left to decay naturally. Fortunately the property is surrounded by thick forest so it gets regular visits from woods-loving birds, including brown creepers, Steller's jays, Swainson's thrushes, and varied thrushes. Pileated woodpeckers also make appearances throughout the year. Even such unusual species as chukar have passed through John's backyard.

He feels it's relatively easy to attract birds to his yard given the setting. "Oregon is still largely rural. Although we are technically still in the town of Scappoose, our home is on an old farm road where the houses are not densely packed and open fields and forests are in abundance. A hundred yards in one direction from us are horses, the same distance in the other direction is a cow field. All one really needs to do here to attract birds is keep a feeder clean, well stocked, and in position and the birds will quickly find it.

"Nature isn't neat and tidy," says John. "Don't over-landscape or keep your property meticulously trimmed and raked. Insects, despite being a pest to your flowers, are also food for the birds you want to attract; without the former, you won't have as many of the latter."

Appendices

Appendix 1: Guide to Boxes for Cavity-Nesting Birds

SPECIES	Interior Floor Size of Box (inches)	Interior Height of Box (inches)	Entrance Hole Diameter (inches)	Box Elevation (feet)
CHICKADEES	4 x 4	9–12	1⅛–1½	5–15
PROTHONOTARY WARBLER	4 x 4	12	1¼	5–12
TITMICE	4 x 4	12	1½	5–12
WHITE-BREASTED NUTHATCH	4 x 4	12	1½	5–12
CAROLINA WRENS	4 x 4	9–12	1–1½	5–10
EASTERN BLUEBIRD	4 x 4	12	1½	5–6
WESTERN BLUEBIRD	5 x 5	12	1½–1⁹⁄₁₆	5–6
MOUNTAIN BLUEBIRD	5 x 5	12	1⁹⁄₁₆	5–6
TREE SWALLOW	5 x 5	10–12	1½	5–10
VIOLET-GREEN SWALLOW	5 x 5	10–12	1½	5–10
PURPLE MARTIN	6 x 6	6	2⅛	15–25
GREAT-CRESTED FLYCATCHER	6 x 6	12	1¾–2	6–20
ASH-THROATED FLYCATCHER	6 x 6	12	1¾–2	6–20
HOUSE FINCH	5 x 5	10	1½	5–10
DOWNY WOODPECKER	4 x 4	12	1½	5–20
HAIRY WOODPECKER	6 x 6	14	1½	8–20
RED-BELLIED WOODPECKER	6 x 6	14	2	8–20
GOLDEN-FRONTED WOODPECKER	6 x 6	14	2	8–20
RED-HEADED WOODPECKER	6 x 6	14	2	8–20
NORTHERN FLICKER	7 x 7	16–24	2½	10–20
PILEATED WOODPECKER	12 x 12	24	4	15–25
BUFFLEHEAD	7 x 7	17	3	5–15
WOOD DUCK	12 x 12	24	3 x 4	5–20
HOODED MERGANSER	12 x 12	24	3 x 4	5–30
GOLDENEYES	12 x 12	24	3¼ x 4¼	15–20
COMMON MERGANSER	12 x 12	24	5 x 6	8–20
SAW-WHET OWL	7 x 7	12	2½	8–20
SCREECH-OWLS	8 x 8	18	3	8–30
BOREAL OWL	8 x 8	18	3	8–30
BARRED OWL	14 x 14	28	8	15–30
BARN OWL	12 x 36	16	6 x 7	15–30
AMERICAN KESTREL	9 x 9	16–18	3	12–30

FOR ALL NEST BOXES: Interior height listed above refers to inside back panel. Always baffle nest boxes. Sizes above are minimum ideal sizes for each species.

FOR WREN BOXES: Larger, oblong holes make it easier to get twigs into box.

FOR SWALLOW BOXES: Carve grooves, or place hardware cloth on inside of front of box.

FOR PURPLE MARTINS: Size listed here is for one compartment in a multi-unit martin house.

Habitat for Box Placement	Comments
Open woods and edges	A 1⅛" hole excludes all other birds except house sparrows.
Wooded swamps and streams	Mount box on a metal pole 5 to 8 feet above open water.
Wooded areas and edge habitat	A 1⅛" hole excludes all other birds except house sparrows.
Wooded areas and edge habitat	Other nuthatch species may prefer a 1¼" hole.
Old fields and thickets	House wrens (1" hole) and Bewick's wrens (1¼" hole).
Open land with scattered trees	
Open land with scattered trees	
Open meadows above 5,000'	
Open land near pond or lake	Place escape ladder on inside front of box. See below.
Pastures, fields, parks	
Open country near water	Entrance hole 1" above the floor. See below.
Open woods and edges	Use a 1⁹⁄₁₆" hole if starlings are a problem.
Open, semi-arid country	
Backyards and porches	Often nests in hanging plants.
Forest openings and edges	
Forest openings and edges	
Forest openings and edges	
Forest openings and edges	
Forest openings and edges	
Farmland, open country	
Mature forest	
Wooded lakeshores, swamps	
Wooded swamps, bottomland	Hole is a horizontally oriented oval.
Wooded swamps, bottomland	
Wooded lakeshores, swamps	
Wooded lakeshores, swamps	
Forest clearings and edges	
Farmland, orchards, woods	
Boreal forests and bogs	
Mature bottomland forest	
Open farmland, marshes	Place box high in barn, silo. Hole should be 4" above floor.
Farmland	

FOR DUCK BOXES: Add 3" of wood chips to floor of box. Staple 5"-wide hardware cloth "ladder" directly under hole on inside of box. Mount boxes higher when not placed over water.

FOR WOODPECKER BOXES: Pack cavity full with wood chips and sawdust.

FOR OWL BOXES: Add 3" of wood chips to floor of box.

NEWLY HATCHED eastern bluebirds.

Appendix 2: Nest-Box Plans

The instructions on the following pages will guide you through the construction of several different nest box or shelf designs, plus a basic pole-mounted predator baffle. Please note the following:

IN REGIONS WITH FREQUENT DAMP WEATHER, nest boxes made from weather-resistant cedar will last longer. Boxes made from other types of wood can be preserved by staining or painting the exterior surfaces annually. Do *not* use pressure-treated wood for nest boxes—it contains chemicals that are toxic to nestlings. While building boxes from plywood is inexpensive and easy, this wood is not nearly as weather-resistant as solid hardwood or cedar.

For all of these box plans, nails can be used to hold pieces together. However, the use of wood screws will make the boxes more sturdy and durable. In some cases it may be easier to pre-drill small holes before inserting screws. On my nest boxes I use galvanized or brass Phillips-head screws and insert them using a cordless power drill. In some cases (such as hinged doors) nails are preferable. Screwed-together nest boxes last longer. Nailed-together boxes may slowly come apart as the wood weathers or ages and shrinks, making it easier for a predator, such as a raccoon, to rip the box open.

When working with tools to build these nest box designs, always keep your own safety in mind. Wear gloves and safety glasses to protect yourself and be extra careful when using power tools.

Basic Bluebird Nest Box

This nest-box design comes from the North American Bluebird Society and is intended to be easy for new landlords (and those who are not experienced woodworkers) to build.

MATERIALS

Standard board for sides, back, floor, front:*
1 inch x 6 inches x 4 feet

Standard board for roof:*
1 inch x 10 inches x 10½ inches

1¾-inch galvanized nails or screws (22)

Double-headed nail for holding door closed (1)

TOOLS

T-square

Pencil

Ruler

Circular saw or hand saw

Rasp or sandpaper

Hammer

Drill, with assorted small bits

Phillips and flathead screwdrivers

* Although standard pine will work for this box, if you live in an area with wet weather, you'll need to paint or stain the outside of the box to prevent the pine roof and walls from admitting moisture. Cedar is more naturally weatherproof, but it can be a bit more expensive.

INSTRUCTIONS

A. Cut the long board as shown in the end board view. Start cutting at the end that will be used for the floor and work your way toward the end that will be used for the back of the box.

B. The dimension of the board used for the back of the box is the least critical from a dimension standpoint (see the diagram labeled "Top Board View").

C. Assemble the cut pieces for the box and sand off any splinters on the inside surfaces. Cut small triangles off the corners of the floor piece to permit drainage and ventilation.

Use the galvanized nails or screws to assemble the box. It may be helpful to use a bench vise or an extra set of hands to hold the pieces in place while joining them. Leave a bit of space (about ⅛ inch) between the roof and the top edge of the sides to allow for ventilation. Recess the floor about ¼ inch into the inside walls so that the sides prevent the open grain of the floor from wicking water into the wood.

A. BOARD DIAGRAM

Start cutting at the "floor" and work
toward the "back" since the back
dimension is the least critical.

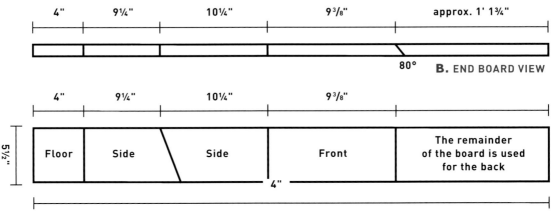

4"   9¼"   10¼"   9³/₈"   approx. 1' 1¾"

80°   **B.** END BOARD VIEW

4"   9¼"   10¼"   9³/₈"

5½"

| Floor | Side | Side | Front | The remainder of the board is used for the back |

4"

TOP BOARD VIEW

C. CONSTRUCTION PLAN

Note: a 1⁹/₁₆" hole
should be used
where the ranges
of eastern or
western blue-
birds overlap with
mountain blue-
birds.

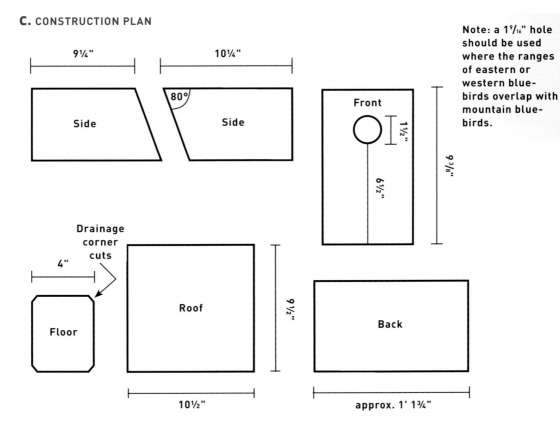

9¼"   10¼"

Side   80°   Side

Front

1½"

9³/₈"

6½"

Drainage
corner
cuts

4"

Floor

Roof   9½"   Back

10½"   approx. 1' 1¾"

D. OPTIONAL OVAL HOLE

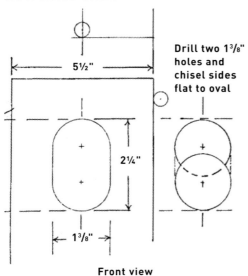

Drill two 1³/₈" holes and chisel sides flat to oval

5½"

2¼"

1³/₈"

Front view

Using the drill, make the entrance hole in the front panel, measuring 1½ inches in diameter.

D. For an oval-shaped entrance, which some bluebird landlords say bluebirds prefer, drill two 1³/₈-inch holes one on top of the other. Chisel or rasp and then sand the excess wood until the entrance sides are smooth. Note: for western and mountain bluebirds, the entrance hole should be 1⁹/₁₆ inches in diameter.

E. Drill a small hole through the front panel and door of the box and insert the double-headed nail to hold the door closed.

Paint or stain the exterior surfaces with latex-based products to preserve the wood and help the box shed water. Mount on a predator-baffled pole in appropriate habitat.

E.

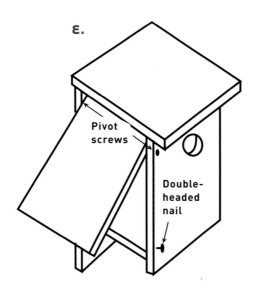

Pivot screws

Double-headed nail

Drill hole through "front" and side of door to hold door closed with nail.

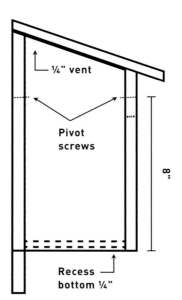

¼" vent

Pivot screws

8"

Recess bottom ¼"

Wren House

This simple wren house is a rather dressy little structure and a great conversation opener. It also requires no beveling—everything fits at right angles!

The house wren does not seem to mind if this house swings a bit in the breeze, from lower branches of a large tree or from a porch or overhanging roof. But these placements make it easier for predators to access the nest, so consider mounting this house on a pole with a predator baffle. Just be certain it is out where wrens can see it.

MATERIALS

Cedar or exterior plywood, ⅝ inch, 18 x 11¼ inches; or T 1-11 siding scraps

Left bottom half—4⅝ x 4 inches

Right bottom half—4 x 4 inches

Back—4⅝ x 4⅝ inches

Front—4⅝ x 4⅝ inches

Roof, left side—8¼ x 5¾ inches

Roof, right side—8¼ x 63/8 inches

Fourpenny galvanized box nails (16–20)

1-inch Phillips-head screws (3)

Caulking compound (1 small tube)

Small eye screws (2), shaft ½ inch from point to eye

Chain or wire, 2 lengths, 12 inches each

TOOLS

T-square

Pencil

Ruler

Hand or circular saw

Plane

Rasp

Hammer

Drill, with assorted small bits

Phillips-head screwdriver

Brace, with 1- or 1½-inch expansion bit and 3/8-inch bit

INSTRUCTIONS

A.

1. Use the T-square and mark out all the parts as shown. Saw out the parts and plane the sawed edges.

2. In the front piece, drill an entrance hole, centered as shown in the diagram, 4¼ inches up from the bottom corner. If this birdhouse is for house or Bewick's wrens, drill a 1-inch hole; if it is for Carolina wrens, drill a 1½-inch hole. Round the edges with a rasp.

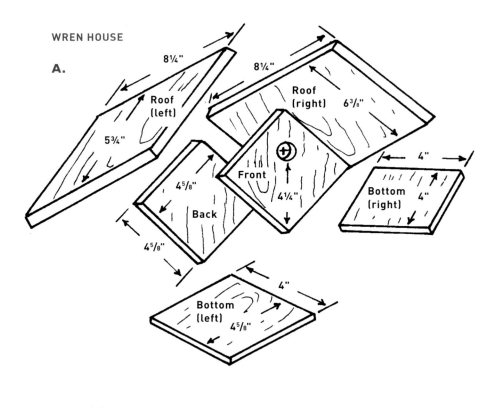

A.

Roof (left) 8¼" 5¾"

Roof (right) 8¼" 6³/₈"

Front 4¼"

Back 4⁵/₈" 4⁵/₈"

Bottom (right) 4" 4"

Bottom (left) 4" 4⁵/₈"

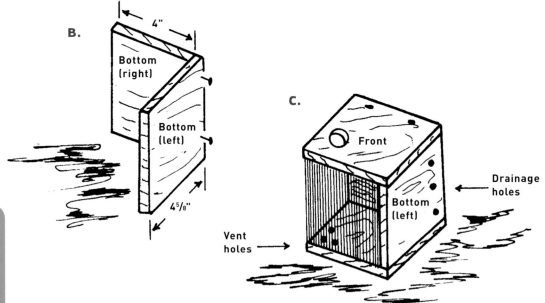

B.

Bottom (right) 4"

Bottom (left) 4⁵/₈"

C.

Front

Bottom (left)

Drainage holes

Vent holes

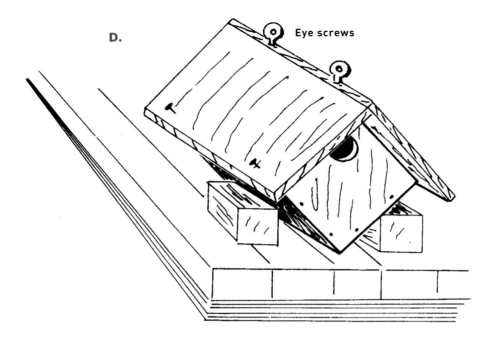

D.

Eye screws

B.

Begin assembly by putting together the two bottom pieces, the larger part overlapping the smaller. Start two nails near the edge of the larger (bottom left) piece and join them as shown. Do not nail all the way.

C.

1. On the workbench, lay the larger (left) piece flat, with a scrap board underneath, allowing the smaller (right) piece to hang over the edge of the bench. Drill three drain holes, each $3/8$ inch in diameter, next to the junction of the two pieces.

2. Near the top corner of the back panel, drill three vent holes, $3/8$ inch in diameter. Place the back in position, vent holes at the top, and tack into the edge of the smaller bottom half. If the fit looks good, drive the nails in.

3. Position the front, and tack two nails for contact with the edge of the smaller bottom half. Check for alignment, then drive the nails in.

D.

1. Lay the unit down on the small half of the roof panel to measure equal overhang, front and back. Mark the position.

Be sure that the temporary nails sticking out of the bottom left panel are toward you, not up.

2. Turn the box over and start two nails in the smaller (left) roof section, near the top of the front and back pieces. Align and drive partway to hold.

3. Check the other half of the roof just for fit, then set it aside. Set two more nails in the smaller half, this time near the bottom of the front and back panels. Do not set any nails in the side, which will be removable. If the panels and nails are straight, drive the nails in.

4. Drill a small hole between the two temporary nails sticking out from the lower end of the bottom left panel. Drill two more holes, one in the front panel and one in the back panel, to connect with the edges of the bottom left piece. Place a screw in each of these three holes to fasten the bottom left panel to the house. Remove the two nails, using a block under the hammer to avoid pulling off the panel. Galvanized nails are the very dickens to pull. This will be the cleanout door. Be sure not to use it for inspecting the nest when the young are present.

5. Run a ribbon of caulking compound along the top edge of the roof joint. Start two nails near the top of the larger (right) roof section, lay it on the house, and drive the nails in, allowing the compound to ooze from the seam. This will seal the house against driving rain. Start two more nails lower down, into the end pieces.

6. Place two eye screws at each end of the roof peak and use two chains or wires to hang the birdhouse 6 to 10 feet above the ground.

Shelf for Barn Swallows, Phoebes, and Robins

This nesting shelf is easy to construct and will be used by barn swallows. Phoebes or robins may be attracted if you add 2 inches to the dimensions of each piece. Since it is so easy to build, you may not mind making two or three. Then you can put up shelves in different locations, increasing your chances of having nesting families.

MATERIALS

Cedar boards or exterior plywood, ⅝ inch, 25¾ x 8¼ inches; or T 1-11 siding scraps:

Bottom—6 x 6 inches

Sides (2)—each 6⅝ x 6 inches

Back—6 x 8 inches

Fourpenny galvanized box nails (12)

Tenpenny galvanized box nails (3)

TOOLS

T-square

Pencil

Ruler

Hand or circular saw and keyhole saw

Plane

Brace, with ½-inch bit

Hammer

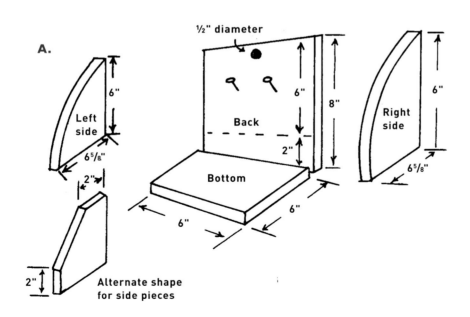

A.

½" diameter

Left side — 6" — 6⅝" — 2"

Back — 6" — 8" — 2"

Right side — 6" — 6⅝"

Bottom — 6" — 6"

2" — Alternate shape for side pieces

A.

1. With a T-square and pencil, lay out and mark the parts according to the dimensions shown in the drawing, then saw out all the pieces. If you do not have a sharp keyhole saw to cut the curve in the end pieces, then make the alternate side pieces, cutting off the corners 2 inches out from the top and 2 inches up from the bottom, as shown. Plane off any splinters.

2. Mark a horizontal line along the face of the back panel, 2 inches up from the bottom. Drill a ½-inch hole, centered in the back and 1 inch down from the top.

3. On the back side (the side that will go against the wall) of the back panel, start two fourpenny nails so they will come out ¼ inch above the line on the other side. Then nail the bottom to the back so that the edges are flush and the underside of the bottom rests on the line drawn on the back piece.

4. Start two fourpenny nails in the right side to connect with the edge of the bottom piece. Start another fourpenny nail in the side panel, 1½ inches from the top, to connect with the back panel. Align the side piece with the bottom and back panels, being sure the edges are flush. Now drive in all the nails. Repeat with the left side panel.

B.   Nails for barn swallow nest

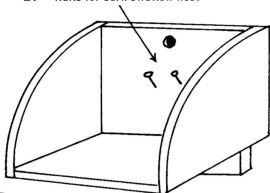

B.

One observer has noticed that barn swallows often anchor their nests to nails on the side of a beam. If you want to test this idea, then put two tenpenny nails into the back panel, about 2 inches apart and 2 inches up from the bottom. Leave 1¾ inches of the nails sticking out.

C.

This shelf nest should be tacked high under the eaves—8 to 12 feet for barn swallows, 6 to 15 feet for phoebes and robins. Drive a tenpenny box nail into the desired location, leaving ¾ inch of the nail protruding. Hook the shelf onto the nail, through the ½-inch hole in the back of the shelf. Where the back extends below the bottom, drive two more fourpenny nails into the back, leaving enough of the nails sticking out so you can pull them easily if you want to try new locations.

C.

These plans are for the largest bird box included in this book. Before starting, be sure that your supply of lumber contains pieces large enough to accommodate the required dimensions. And don't forget the 4 inches of wood chips in the bottom. It's a very important cushion for the eggs.

MATERIALS

Cedar, pine, or exterior plywood, ⅝ inch, 55 x 37¼ inches; or T 1-11 siding scraps:

Bottom—10½ x 10½ inches

Sides (2)—each 27¾ x 27 x 10½ inches

Back—31 x 11¾ inches

Front—27 x 11¾ inches

Roof—14 x 14 inches

Fourpenny galvanized box nails (24 or a large handful)

Galvanized hardware cloth, ¼-inch mesh, 4 x 19 inches

Staples, #5, wire brad

Cleats (2)—board, 1 x 4 x 10¼ inches, ripped in half to make each cleat 1 by 1¾ x 10¼ inches

Screen-door hooks and eyes (2 pairs)

Sixteenpenny galvanized framing nails (3)

Galvanized pipe, 1½ inches; long enough to extend 4 feet above water

Threaded pipe flange

Flathead or Phillips screws, #8, ¾ inch (6)

Strap iron, 2 pieces, each 30 inches long, 3¾ inches wide, ⅛–³⁄₁₆ inch thick

Metal hose clamp, ¼ inches in diameter

Wood chips, enough to fill space that is 4 x 10½ x 10½ inches

TOOLS

T-square

Pencil

Ruler

Hand or circular saw

Rasp

Plane

Compass, or 3-inch jar lid

Hammer

Phillips-head and flathead screwdriver

Brace, with 3-inch expansion bit, or ⅝-inch bit and keyhole saw

A.

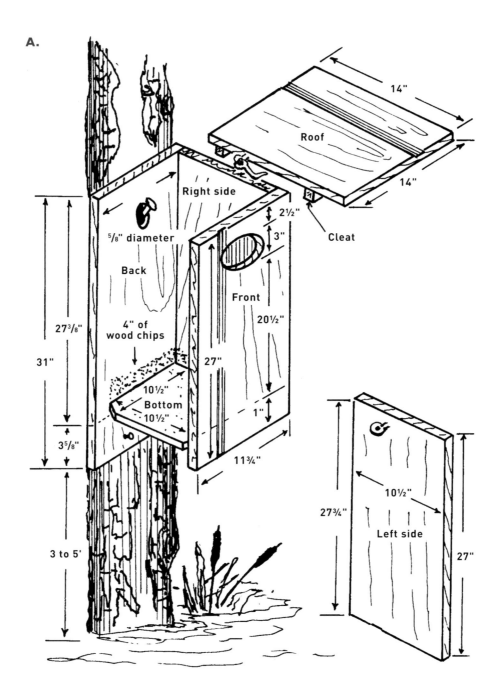

Roof

14"

14"

Right side

2½"

3"

Cleat

⅝" diameter

Back

Front

4" of
wood chips

20½"

27⅜"

27"

31"

10½"

Bottom

1"

10½"

3⅝"

11¾"

3 to 5'

27¾"

10½"

Left side

27"

A.

1. Check over the dimensions. With a T-square and a pencil, lay out all the parts on the weather (outside-facing) surface, with grooves running down the sides and slope of the roof, not across. Then saw out all the pieces. Be sure the corners of the bottom are cut off $\frac{5}{8}$ inch back. Drill a $\frac{5}{8}$-inch hole, centered in the back panel, 2 inches down from the top. Bevel the back and front panels $\frac{1}{8}$ inch at the top to accommodate the roof slant.

2. On the front panel, center a 4- x 3-inch rectangle 2½ inches down from the top, as shown in the drawing, but remember that you beveled off $\frac{1}{8}$ inch and allow for it. Use a compass or 3-inch jar lid to circumscribe a semicircle at each end of the rectangle. Use a 3-inch expansion bit to cut the ends of the rectangle. If you do not have an expansion bit, then drill a $\frac{5}{8}$-inch hole just inside the curve and cut out the entrance with a keyhole saw to give the opening an elliptical shape. Round off the edges with a rasp.

3. Draw a line across the interior surface of the back panel, $3\frac{5}{8}$ inches up from the bottom. Extend it over the edge and across the weather surface. (This is to match up with the outside surface of the bottom panel.) Next, draw a line across the interior surface of the right side panel, 1 inch up from the bottom. Extend it across the edges and the weather surface. Put one more line, 1 inch up from the bottom, across the interior surface of the front panel, and extend it across the edges and the weather surface.

4. Start the assembly by putting two nails in the right side panel, to come out ¼ inch below the line on the other side. Place the bottom on edge. Lay the side panel across with the line marked on it matching the interior surface of the bottom panel. Be sure the edges are flush by sliding the two pieces against a wall. Drive the nails partway in.

5. Turn the joined pieces on the side edge. Position the back, matching its line with the outside surface of the bottom and making its top flush with the side panel. Put three nails through the back, into the edge of the side. Drive the nails partway in. The back should extend $3\frac{5}{8}$ inches below the bottom panel. The side should slope evenly, its top edge matching the top of the back and front panels. Hold the front panel in position and check it.

6. Put a nail through the back near the outer corner of the bottom, line it up, hold, and drive the nail partway in. Put another nail into the inside corner. Look over the alignment. If it is good, drive in all the nails.

7. You are now ready for the front, but first let's get the hardware cloth nailed on the inside so you won't have to crawl in and do it later. Tack a 4-inch width of hardware cloth, 19 inches long, from the edge of the entrance to within 1½ inches of the floor. You can tack the material flat using staples and a hammer (a staple gun is fine if you have one). Make sure you do not leave *any* rough ends or edges exposed that might scratch or cut the birds.

8. Position the front, the bottom of it even with the side panel. Put three nails through the front, partway into the edge of the side panel. Line up the bottom, hold, and put one nail through the front into the outside corner. Put one more nail into the inside corner, but keep in mind that the corners have been cut back—don't get your nails too close. Check the alignment, then drive in all the nails.

9. Slip the left side into place. Line it up and nail it—three nails into the front panel, three into the back, and two along the bottom.

10. The roof on this house is removable so you can inspect the nest and clean out the box. Lay the top in position, the rear portion flush with the back. Slide it 2 or 3 inches to one side and mark the inside of the roof along the edges of the front and back panels. Draw lines across at these marks inside the roof, paralleling the front and back. These lines are used to line up the front and back cleats.

11. To make two cleats, take a 1- x 4-inch board, 10¼ inches long. Down the center, ripsaw two pieces, about 1¾ inches wide. Check the length inside the box. If the cleats are too long, shave the ends a bit. Place them an equal distance from either edge of the top piece and nail them just inside the lines. Clinch the nails if they come through.

12. Check the top for fit. Set screen-door hooks and eyes on each side to hold it firm.

13. You can mount this box in the same manner as other slant-roof boxes. First, drive a sixteenpenny galvanized framing nail, angled downward, into a tree or snag. Leave 1½ inches sticking out. Hook the box through the hole in the back. Place two more sixteenpenny nails into the extension, beneath, but do not drive them all the way in. This is an advantage. With a small wrecking bar you can quickly pull the nails and relocate the box if necessary.

B.

1. You can place wood duck boxes in farm ponds by incorporating 1½-inch galvanized pipe, driven deep into the mud bottom, to extend 4 feet above the surface of the water. Underneath the bottom of the box, center a threaded pipe flange and fasten it with screws. Rotate the box onto the pipe threads on top of the pipe.

2. Extra bracing may include two pieces of strap iron, fastened to the sides with screws. Angle them inward beneath, then secure them to the pipe with a metal hose clamp. Painting will hold off rusting. In snake country, leave the braces off.

B.

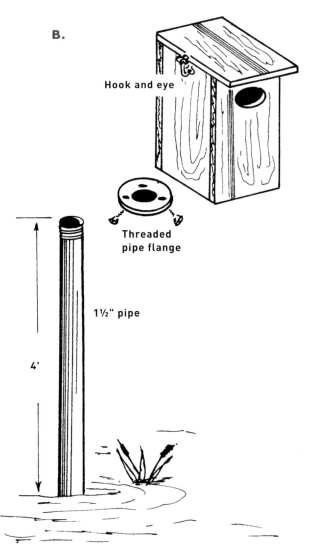

Hook and eye

Threaded
pipe flange

1½" pipe

4'

Screech-owl and Kestrel Box

This simple box will work for screech-owls as well as kestrels when put up in appropriate habitat. The procedure for building it is much the same as that used for the wood duck box, except that this house has a hinge-nail side opening instead of a removable top.

MATERIALS

Cedar boards or exterior plywood, ⅝ inch, 45 x 27¼ inches; or T 1-11 siding scraps:

Bottom—8 x 8 inches

Sides (2)—each 15¾ x 14¾ x 8 inches

Back—19 x 9¼ inches

Front—15 x 9¼ inches

Roof—11¼ x 11¼ inches

Fourpenny galvanized box nails (24 or a large handful)

Galvanized nail or right-angle screw hook, either one about 1½ inches long

Caulking compound (1 small tube)

Sixteenpenny galvanized framing nail (1)

Galvanized siding nails (2)

TOOLS

T-square

Pencil

Ruler

Hand or circular saw

Plane

Rasp

Hammer

Keyhole saw, or brace with 3-inch expansion bit and ½-inch bit

A.

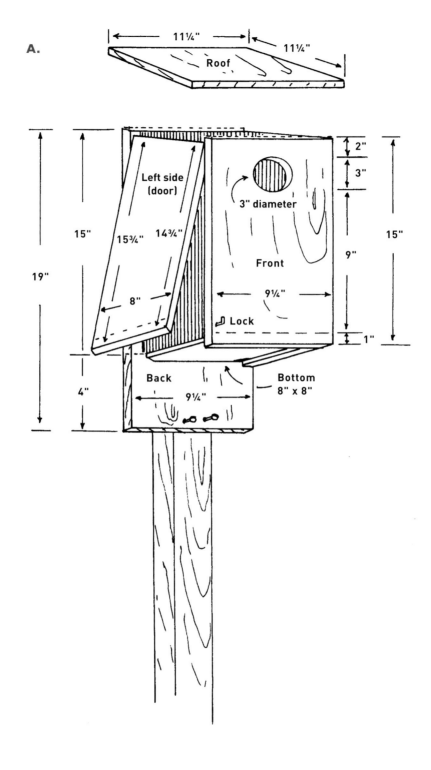

11¼" 11¼"

Roof

2"

3"

3" diameter

Left side
(door)

Front

15" 15¾" 14¾"

9"

15"

19"

8"

9¼"

🔒 Lock

1"

Back

Bottom
8" x 8"

4"

9¼"

A.

1. Lay out, mark, and saw out all the parts.

2. On the back panel, drill a ½-inch hole, centered 2 inches down from the top.

3. On the front panel, cut out the 3-inch entrance, centered 2 inches down from the top, as shown.

4. Bevel ⅛ inch off the back and front pieces to fit the roof slant.

5. Across the interior surface of the back, 4 inches up from the bottom, draw a line, extending it across the edges and the weather (outside-facing) surface. Draw another line across the interior surface of the right side panel, 1 inch up from the bottom, and extend it across the edges. Do the same with the front panel.

6. If the wood is smooth, roughen the interior surfaces of the front and side panels with the corner of the rasp, scratching hard across the grain. Chiseled-out grooves on the inside front of the nest box, below the entrance hole, will help ducklings depart safely at fledging time.

7. Put two nails into the right side, to come out ¼ inch below the line on the interior surface. Set the bottom on edge. Match the line on the right side panel with the interior surface of the bottom panel. Push both pieces flush against a wall, and drive the nails partway in.

8. Turn the unit on its side edge. Put two nails into the back to connect with the edge of the right side panel. Match the marks as you fit the two pieces together. Drive the nails partway in. Check to see if the back extends ¼ inch above the side panel. Line up the bottom, hold, and drive two nails partway in. If everything fits, drive in all the nails.

9. Place the front in position, matching the marks. See if it extends ¼ inch above the right side panel. Put two nails into the side and two into the bottom. Check the alignment, then drive them all in.

10. Slip the other side in place to check for fit. Draw a horizontal line, 1 inch from the top, across the weather surface. Put one nail through the front panel and one nail through the back panel, at either end of the line. Drill a hole near the bottom for the nail—a 1½-inch galvanized nail or right-angle screw hook (this is the "lock" shown in the illustration).

11. Run a strip of caulking compound along the beveled edge of the back panel. Position the roof so it is flush with the back and has an equal overhang on each side. Put two nails in back and two in front.

B.

To mount this box, drive a sixteenpenny galvanized nail into the place you have chosen for the box, being sure that it hangs 6 to 20 feet above the ground (12 to 30 feet for kestrels). Hook the house on this nail, through the ½-inch hole in back, then drive two galvanized siding nails partway through the back, where it extends beneath the bottom. Leave the nails sticking out enough that you can pull them out easily when changing locations.

B.

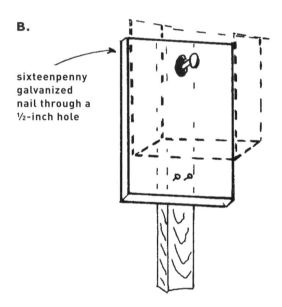

sixteenpenny
galvanized
nail through a
½-inch hole

The Gilbertson Baffle and Pole Mount

MATERIALS

Aluminum electrical conduit, ½ inch diameter x 5 feet long

#4 iron rebar, ½ inch x 5 feet

½-inch conduit connectors (2)

¾-inch machine screws (flat head) (2)

½-inch strapping brackets and weatherproof screws (to mount box to pole)

Duct tape, hanger iron (in two 7-inch strips)

Machine screws with nuts for hanger iron (2)

Galvanized stovepipe (34 inches x 7 inches) with 7-inch steel cap

TOOLS

Mallet

Phillips and flat-head screwdrivers

Needle-nose pliers

Crescent wrench

Knock-out punch (for ½-inch conduit [hole size .89 inch], to make a neat hole in the stovepipe cap to accommodate the pipe)

THIS ILLUSTRATION shows a bluebird's-eye-view of a raccoon and the stovepipe baffle mount. The slick metal baffle wobbles on the pole, preventing snakes and climbing animals from reaching the box. Baffle and pole mount designed by Steve Gilbertson.

INSTRUCTIONS

1. With a mallet, drive the 5-foot length of iron rebar halfway into the ground. Drop a ½-inch conduit connector over the top of the rebar, and replace the lower screw in it with a ¾-inch machine screw. This connector serves as a sleeve to affix the conduit firmly to its supporting rebar, and it prevents swiveling. Slip the 5-foot length of conduit over the rebar; the rebar serves to support the conduit. Tighten both screws—the lower screw into the rebar and the top screw into the conduit.

2. Using the knockout punch, make a hole in the center of the stovepipe cap. Bend and crimp the stovepipe into a cylinder. Fit the cap into the knurled end of the stovepipe.

3. Hold the nest box up at the height it will be mounted. A few inches beneath the box, run a double strip of duct tape around the conduit pipe. Use the machine screws and nuts to tighten the two strips of hanger iron securely around the duct tape, on either side of the mounting pipe, and bend them into an X shape as shown. Slip the assembled baffle over the top of the pipe and down onto the hanger iron bracket, just below where the nest box will hang (the higher on the pole, the better). It should wobble a little, which will further discourage climbing predators. Now mount the nest box using the strapping brackets. You're done!

Resources

Books

Donnelly, David B. *Creating Your Backyard Bird Garden*. Marietta, OH: Bird Watcher's Digest Press, 1998, 2008.

Ehrlich, Paul R., David S. Dobkin, and Darryl Wheye. *The Birder's Handbook: A Field Guide to the Natural History of North American Birds*. New York, NY: Simon and Schuster, 1988.

Laubach, René, and Christyna M. Laubach. *The Backyard Birdhouse Book*. North Adams, MA: Storey Books, 1998.

Shalaway, Scott. *A Guide to Bird Homes*. Marietta, OH: Bird Watcher's Digest Press, 2010.

Stokes, Donald, and Lillian Stokes. *The Complete Birdhouse Book*. Boston, MA: Little Brown, 1990.

Thompson, Bill, III. *The Backyard Bird Watcher's Answer Guide*. Marietta, OH: Bird Watcher's Digest Press, 2009.

Thompson, Bill, III. *Identifying and Feeding Birds*. Boston, MA: Houghton Mifflin Harcourt, 2010.

Thompson, Bill, III, and Connie Toops. *Hummingbirds and Butterflies*. Boston, MA: Houghton Mifflin Harcourt, 2011.

Wolinski, Richard A. *Enjoying Purple Martins More*. Marietta, OH: Bird Watcher's Digest Press, 1994.

Zickefoose, Julie. *Enjoying Bluebirds More*. Marietta, OH: Bird Watcher's Digest Press, 2009.

Zickefoose, Julie. *Backyard Birding: Using Natural Gardening to Attract Birds*. New York, NY: Skyhorse Publishing, 2011.

Organizations

National Audubon Society
225 Varick Street, New York, NY 10014
www.audubon.org; also web4.audubon.org/bird/at_home/
HealthyYard_BirdHabitat.html

National Wildlife Federation
Backyard Habitat Program
11100 Wildlife Center Drive, Reston VA 20190
www.nwf.org/Get-Outside/Outdoor-Activities/Garden-
for-Wildlife.aspx

National Wildlife Rehabilitators Association
2625 Clearwater Road, Suite 110 , St. Cloud, MN 56301
www.nwrawildlife.org/content/finding-rehabilitator

The Nature Conservancy
4245 North Fairfax Drive, Suite 100, Arlington, VA 22203
www.nature.org

EVEN A flower bed can provide a bit of cover for backyard birds.

BIRD-FRIENDLY BACKYARDS *make for great birdwatching!*

NestWatch

Cornell Lab of Ornithology, 159 Sapsucker Woods Road, Ithaca, NY 14850

www.nestwatch.org

North American Bluebird Society

P.O. Box 7844, Bloomington, IN 47407

www.nabluebirdsociety.org

North American Native Plant Society

P.O. Box 84, Station D, Etobicoke, ON M9A 4X1 CANADA

www.nanps.org

Purple Martin Conservation Association

301 Peninsula Drive, Suite 6, Erie, PA 16505

www.purplemartin.org

The Purple Martin Society, NA

21250 South Redwood Lane, Suite 101, Shorewood, IL 60404

www.purplemartins.com

A MALE eastern bluebird.

Photography and Illustration Credits

Bird Watchers Digest: 47 bottom, 174 top, 174 bottom, 175, 177, 178, 179, 181, 184 bottom, 186, 188, 189

Louise Chambers/PMCA: 44

Dudley Edmondson: 145 top, 145 bottom left, 145 bottom right, 146 top, 146 bottom, 147 top, 147 bottom

Steve and Cheryl Eno: 71, 148 top, 148 bottom, 149 top, 149 bottom, 150

Marci Fuller: 142 top, 142 bottom left, 142 bottom right, 143 top left, 143 top right, 143 middle, 143 bottom, 144 top left, 144 top right, 144 bottom

Lynn Hassler: 151 top, 151 bottom, 152 top, 152 bottom

Alvaro Jaramillo: 160, 161, 162 top, 162 bottom

John and Durrae Johnson: 157 top, 157 bottom left, 157 bottom right, 158 top, 158 bottom, 159 top, 159 bottom

Ed Kanze: 49, 121, 122

Andy Kinsey: 138 left, 138 right, 139 top, 139 bottom, 140, 141

Robert McCaw: 57, 96

Dave Maslowski: xiii, 8, 32, 35 top, 46 bottom, 50, 56, 58, 67, 72, 74, 76 top, 81, 82, 84 left, 84 right, 85, 88, 89, 107, 116, 118

Claire Mullen/BWD: 120

North American Bluebird Society: 171 top, 171 bottom, 172 top, 172 bottom

Jeff Payne: 126 top, 126 bottom, 127 top, 127 bottom

Alan Pulley: 128 top, 128 bottom left, 128 bottom right, 129 top, 129 middle, 129 bottom left, 129 bottom right, 130 top left, 130 top right, 130 bottom

John Riutta: 163 top, 163 bottom, 164 top left, 164 top right, 164 bottom

Bill Schmoker: 46 top, 75, 78

Clay and Pat Sutton: 123 top, 123 middle, 123 bottom, 124, 125 top, 125 middle, 125 bottom

Bill Thompson III: vi, viii, x, xi, xii, 2, 3, 4, 5, 6, 9, 10, 11, 13, 15, 17 top, 17 bottom, 19, 20, 21, 22, 23 bottom, 26, 28, 29, 30, 31, 33, 34, 35 bottom, 36, 37, 38, 39 top, 39 bottom, 40, 42, 45, 47 top, 51 top, 51 bottom, 52, 53, 62, 63, 64, 68, 70, 76 bottom, 86, 92, 93, 94, 95 top, 95 bottom, 97, 98, 99, 100, 101, 105, 111, 113, 114, 115, 132 top left, 132 top right, 133 top left, 133 top right, 134, 165, 169, 192, 193, 196

Phoebe Linnea Thompson: 131 bottom right

Connie Toops: 135 top, 135 middle, 135 bottom, 136, 137 top, 137 bottom, 194

Kathy Wiederholt: 153 top, 153 bottom left, 153 bottom right, 154 top, 154 bottom, 155

Julie Zickefoose: xiv–1, 7, 23 top, 25, 41, 48, 54 top, 54 bottom (all), 55, 59, 60, 66, 69, 72, 73, 79, 83, 90, 91, 102, 103, 106, 112, 119, 131 top left, 131 top right, 131 bottom left, 132 bottom, 133 bottom, 168

Julie Zickefoose/Bird Watchers Digest: 184 top, 185

BLACK-EYED SUSANS *produce tiny seeds that finches and sparrows eat in fall and winter.*

Index

Page references in italic refer to species profiles.